W9-AVP-990

RIVER FOREST JR/SR
HIGH SCHOOL LIBRARY

DATE DUE

SEP 1 7 2015	
	PRINTED IN U.S.A.

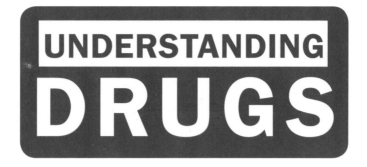

Date Rape Drugs

TITLES IN THE *UNDERSTANDING DRUGS* SERIES

UNDERSTANDING DRUGS

Date Rape Drugs

SUELLEN MAY

CONSULTING EDITOR
DAVID J. TRIGGLE, PH.D.
University Professor
School of Pharmacy and Pharmaceutical Sciences
State University of New York at Buffalo

CHELSEA HOUSE
An Infobase Learning Company

Chelsea House
An imprint of Infobase Learning
132 West 31st Street
New York, NY 10001

Library of Congress Cataloging-in-Publication Data

May, Suellen.
  Date Rape Drugs / Suellen May ; consulting editor David J. Triggle.
    p. cm. — (Understanding drugs)
  Includes bibliographical references and index.
  ISBN-13: 978-1-60413-537-4 (hardcover : alk. paper)
  ISBN-10: 1-60413-537-9 (hardcover : alk. paper)   1. Date rape drugs.   2. Date
    Rape.   I. Title.   II. Series.
  HV6558.M29   2011
  362.883—dc22   2010049628

Chelsea House books are available at special discounts when purchased in bulk quantities for businesses, associations, institutions, or sales promotions. Please call our Special Sales Department in New York at (212) 967-8800 or (800) 322-8755.

You can find Chelsea House on the World Wide Web at
http://www.chelseahouse.com

Text design by Kerry Casey
Cover design by Alicia Post
Composition by Newgen
Cover printed by Bang Printing, Brainerd, Minn.
Book printed and bound by Bang Printing, Brainerd, Minn.
Date printed: February 2011
Printed in the United States of America

10 9 8 7 6 5 4 3 2 1

This book is printed on acid-free paper.

All links and Web addresses were checked and verified to be correct at the time of publication. Because of the dynamic nature of the Web, some addresses and links may have changed since publication and may no longer be valid.

Contents

foreword

THE USE AND ABUSE OF DRUGS

For thousands of years, humans have used a variety of sources with which to cure their ills, cast out devils, promote their well-being, relieve their misery, and control their fertility. Until the beginning of the twentieth century, the agents used were all of natural origin, including many derived from plants as well as elements such as antimony, sulfur, mercury, and arsenic. The sixteenth-century alchemist and physician Paracelsus used mercury and arsenic in his treatment of syphilis, worms, and other diseases that were common at that time; his cure rates, however, remain unknown. Many drugs used today have their origins in natural products. Antimony derivatives, for example, are used in the treatment of the nasty tropical disease leishmaniasis. These plant-derived products represent molecules that have been "forged in the crucible of evolution" and continue to supply the scientist with molecular scaffolds for new drug development.

Our story of modern drug discovery may be considered to start with the German physician and scientist Paul Ehrlich, often called the father of chemotherapy. Born in 1854, Ehrlich became interested in the ways in which synthetic dyes, then becoming a major product of the German fine chemical industry, could selectively stain certain tissues and components of cells. He reasoned that such dyes might form the basis for drugs that could interact selectively with diseased or foreign cells and organisms. One of Ehrlich's early successes was development of the arsenical "606"—patented under the name *Salvarsan*—as a treatment for syphilis. Ehrlich's goal was to create a "magic bullet," a drug that would target only the diseased cell or the invading disease-causing organism and have no effect on healthy cells and tissues. In this he was not successful, but his great research did lay the groundwork for the successes of the twentieth century, including the discovery of the sulfonamides and the antibiotic penicillin. The latter agent saved countless lives during World War II. Ehrlich, like many scientists, was an optimist. On the eve of World War I, he wrote, "Now that the liability to, and danger of, disease are to a large extent circumscribed—the efforts of chemotherapeutics are directed as far as possible to fill up the gaps left in this ring." As we shall see in the pages of this volume, it is neither the first nor the last time that science has proclaimed its victory over nature, only to have to see this optimism dashed in the light of some freshly emerging infection.

From these advances, however, has come the vast array of drugs that are available to the modern physician. We are increasingly close to Ehrlich's magic bullet: Drugs can now target very specific molecular defects in a number of cancers, and doctors today have the ability to investigate the human genome to more effectively match the drug and the patient. In the next one to two decades, it is almost certain that the cost of "reading" an individual genome will be sufficiently cheap that, at least in the developed world, such personalized medicines will become the norm. The development of such drugs, however, is extremely costly and raises significant social issues, including equity in the delivery of medical treatment.

The twenty-first century will continue to produce major advances in medicines and medicine delivery. Nature is, however, a resilient foe. Diseases and organisms develop resistance to existing drugs, and new drugs must constantly be developed. (This is particularly true for anti-infective and anticancer agents.) Additionally, new and more lethal forms of existing infectious diseases can develop rapidly. With the ease of global travel, these can spread from Timbuktu to Toledo in less than 24 hours and become pandemics. Hence the current concerns with avian flu. Also, diseases that have previously been dormant or geographically circumscribed may suddenly break out worldwide. (Imagine, for example, a worldwide pandemic of Ebola disease, with public health agencies totally overwhelmed.) Finally, there are serious concerns regarding the possibility of man-made epidemics occurring through the deliberate or accidental spread of disease agents—including manufactured agents, such as smallpox with enhanced lethality. It is therefore imperative that the search for new medicines continue.

All of us at some time in our life will take a medicine, even if it is only aspirin for a headache or to reduce cosmetic defects. For some individuals, drug use will be constant throughout life. As we age, we will likely be exposed to a variety of medications—from childhood vaccines to drugs to relieve pain caused by a terminal disease. It is not easy to get accurate and understandable information about the drugs that we consume to treat diseases and disorders. There are, of course, highly specialized volumes aimed at medical or scientific professionals. These, however, demand a sophisticated knowledge base and experience to be comprehended. Advertising on television is widely available but provides only fleeting information, usually about only a single drug and designed to market rather than inform. The intent of this series of books, **Understanding Drugs**, is to provide the lay reader with intelligent, readable, and accurate descriptions of drugs, why and how they are used, their limitations, their side effects, and their future. The series will discuss both *"treatment drugs"*—typically, but not exclusively, prescription drugs, that have well-established criteria of both efficacy and safety—and *"drugs of abuse,"* agents that have pronounced pharmacological and physiological effects but that are, for a variety of reasons, not to be considered for therapeutic purposes. It is our hope that these books will provide readers with sufficient information to satisfy their immediate needs and to serve as an adequate base for further investigation and for asking intelligent questions of health care providers.

—David J. Triggle, Ph.D.
University Professor
School of Pharmacy and Pharmaceutical Sciences
State University of New York at Buffalo

1
Introduction: Date Rape Drugs

In February Leah met Jeff through an online dating Web site. Jeffrey came across as confident and interesting as he described life as an emergency room (ER) surgeon. After exchanging e-mails online, Leah agreed to meet Jeff at a downtown restaurant. At times during the conversation, Leah thought the tall, blue-eyed Jeff was a little full of himself. Still, she was having a much better time than she had on her other online dates.

While at dinner, Leah, a 28-year-old accountant, drank a beer and then had another. After four hours of dining, Jeff ordered a carafe of wine while Leah excused herself to the ladies' room. Leah was not surprised to see her glass of wine already poured for her when she returned. She thought it was consistent with Jeff's gentlemanly behavior. But Jeff had dropped a date rape drug into her drink at dinner, earlier that night. After her first sip, the next thing Leah remembered was Jeff having sex with her in a dark room. She was unable to move her legs or arms and her mind felt murky. She tried to mutter a protest but Jeffrey just laughed. Leah came in and out of consciousness during the night to experience Jeff violating her.

DATE RAPE DRUGS DEFINED

Gamma hydroxybutyrate (**GHB**), **ketamine**, and **Rohypnol** are the three main types of drugs referred to as date rape drugs. Alcohol, however, is by far the most common drug used to facilitate date rape. Although each of these drugs differs in their effect on the body, they all act as sedatives, often causing unconsciousness and amnesia. They are easily dissolved in liquids, particularly alcohol, and thus can be consumed unknowingly. A perpetrator may place a date rape drug in a person's drink, rendering the victim unconscious. The primary motivation for illicitly administering date rape drugs, is, as the name implies, sexual assault, particularly since amnesia increases the chances that the assailant is never caught.

Another effect of these drugs is **euphoria**, which makes them popular drugs for recreational use at nightclubs and raves, particularly when consumed with alcohol or other drugs to increase the intoxicating effect. Heroin addicts use Rohypnol to prolong the effects of heroin or in combination with methadone or codeine. In the case of ketamine, users also enjoy the hallucinations that accompany the drug. **Hallucinations** are significant distortions of reality where a person believes they are seeing, feeling, and hearing images, sensations, and sounds that are not real.

THE PREVALENCE OF DRUG-FACILITATED DATE RAPE

Statistics vary considerably on the actual occurrence of drug-facilitated date rape. The reason for this discrepancy is the difficulty in proving drug-facilitated date rape versus date rape through alcohol. Alcohol is considered a drug and many experts believe alcohol is the most common date rape drug; however, a distinction is made, both legally and biologically, by using a drug such as GHB, ketamine, or Rohypnol to rape someone.

There are two categories of drug-facilitated date rape. One category is when a perpetrator surreptitiously slips a date rape drug into someone's drink. Another category consists of people who take one of these drugs of their own volition but then pass out and are taken advantage of sexually. Rape is nonconsensual sex, and if the person (usually a woman) is passed out, then consent cannot take place. Women who take Rohypnol, GHB, or ketamine recreationally are at a much higher risk of date rape.

For those women who do not voluntarily take these drugs, a typical scenario of drug-facilitated date rape is as follows: A woman drinks, feels her level of intoxication far surpasses what she recalls drinking, but hesitates in reporting her suspicions as rape. In many cases, she might have very limited, or no, memory of the sexual assault. These victims often wake up in strange locations and partially dressed with little to no knowledge of how they got there. If they do recall, it is often a cloudy memory of being paralyzed and powerless. If a victim delays reporting the rape, the drugs, if present, will be eliminated from the body. In many cases, women will come forward with an allegation of rape but there is essentially no evidence to prove that they were drugged. Some professionals tend to dismiss these allegations and others believe that the prevalence of drug-facilitated rape is underreported due to the scenario depicted. According to a 2006 report by the British Association of Chief Police Officers, in a study of 120 cases of alleged drug-facilitated sexual assault, scientists found that GHB was used in two cases. Scientists suspected that date-rape drugs had been used in 10 cases and could not rule out that the victims' drinks had been spiked in a further 11 cases.[1] Of the 120 cases, 119 of the women reported drinking alcohol. Rohypnol was not detected in any of the victims' blood or urine. Interestingly, some experts, such as the authors of a study published in the *British Journal of Criminology,* took this report to mean that date rape is nothing more than an "urban myth" and went further to state that "there is a stark contrast between heightened perceptions of risk associated with drug-facilitated sexual assault and a lack of evidence that this is a widespread threat."[2] Many women's advocacy groups viewed the report with skepticism.

Although the study shows that the evidence proving drug-facilitated date rape is relatively low, it still reveals that in two of the cases GHB was used to drug the women. Even a relatively low incidence of drugging should be enough to caution women against leaving their drinks unattended. Rape is a devastating experience and if it happens to an individual the impacts are not lessened by how common or uncommon the event is to women at large.

Date rape drugs are used not only on strangers during a date or evening out at a bar. They are also used on wives, children, and teens to facilitate rape. In March 2002 a South Dakota man purchased a dietary supplement from a Canadian company over the Internet. It contained **1,4-Butanediol (1,4-BD** or **BD)**, a drug that converts to GHB in the body. On several occasions, the man put BD in his wife's alcoholic drink and then sexually assaulted her. She later testified to having a vague recollection of the events. Even if two people are married, nonconsensual sex is rape. On another evening, the wife and husband had separate plans that took them away from the home, so they hired a babysitter to watch their children. The wife arrived home later that evening to

Figure 1.1   The addition of a sedative such as Rohypnol, ketamine, or GHB to an alcoholic beverage is a common method by which perpetrators immobilize their victims.   (© *Monkey Business Images/Shutterstock*)

find her husband with a very drowsy babysitter. The babysitter claimed that the husband gave her something for her headache and she then recalled him rubbing her back and breasts. The wife took the babysitter to the hospital, filed a complaint, and the husband was arrested for possession of BD and the distribution of BD to a minor.[3]

BENZODIAZEPINES: THE ANTIANXIETY AGENTS

Benzodiazepines, often referred simply as benzos, are a group of drugs known for their sedating effect. Benzodiazepines, such as Valium (diazepam), Ativan (lorazepam), Rohypnol (*flunitrazepam*), and Xanax (alprazolam), are classified as depressants that act on the **central nervous system** to reduce pain and anxiety, lower inhibitions, slow breathing, pulse, decrease blood pressure and cause poor concentration. The central nervous system consists of the brain, nerves, and spinal cord, and is responsible for issuing nerve impulses and analyzing data. If suddenly a hiker sees a bear along a trail, the central nervous system enables the hiker to analyze this image, process it, and react appropriately. An impaired or depressed central nervous system reduces appropriate reaction times, among other things.

Benzodiazepines also cause confusion, dizziness, impair coordination, increase fatigue, depress the respiratory system, and impair memory and judgment. Benzodiazepines can be highly addictive both physically and psychologically. The psychological component of the addiction comes from the ability of the benzos to relieve any stress or worries. Users also might find that they are so physically addicted that they can no longer fall asleep without taking a benzo. Many benzos are prescribed legally prior to or following surgery, or during periods of stress. For many people, this is their first introduction to the tranquilizing effect that these drugs have, and some people begin to abuse the drugs at this point. Many who abuse benzos will visit various doctors to get an excessive amount of prescriptions filled, or purchase these drugs on the Internet or the black market.

ROHYPNOL: A FAST-ACTING BENZO

Rohypnol, commonly called roofies, R-2s, the forget-me pill, and roches dos on the streets, is a drug in the benzodiazepine family that was first developed in the1960s. It was marketed as Rohypnol in 1975 as a treatment for insomnia. Manufactured by Hoffman-Roche Pharmaceuticals, Rohypnol is also used to induce sedation and as a preanesthetic. Rohypnol has an effect similar to Valium but is much more potent, essentially five to 10 times stronger than Valium. Rohypnol is metabolized and passed out of the body relatively quickly. Rohypnol has no taste or odor. Rohypnol is used as a potent sleeping pill. The drug slows motor responses, relaxes muscles, and causes amnesia. Rohypnol causes sedation in 20 to 30 minutes with an oral dose of 1 to 2 mg.

Rohypnol dissolves easily in carbonated beverages. The sedative and toxic effects of Rohypnol are increased when taken with alcohol. Even without alcohol, doses as small as 1 milligram can incapacitate a victim for eight to 12 hours.

Rohypnol is illegal in the United States and Canada but is legal in more than 62 countries in Europe and Latin America as a treatment for severe insomnia under the trade names Hipnosedon, Hypnodorm, Flunipam, Nilium, Vulbegal, Silece, Darkene, Ilman and Insom. Legally prescribed, the

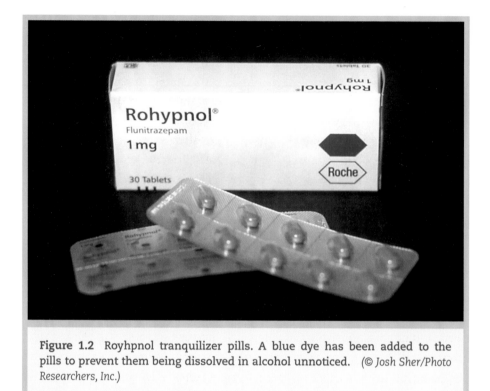

Figure 1.2 Royhpnol tranquilizer pills. A blue dye has been added to the pills to prevent them being dissolved in alcohol unnoticed. *(© Josh Sher/Photo Researchers, Inc.)*

drug comes in a 1-milligram dose in an olive green, oblong tablet, imprinted with the number 542.

According to the National Institute on Drug Abuse, in 1995 Rohypnol was the most widely prescribed sedative-hypnotic in western Europe, with more than 2.3 million doses sold worldwide each day.[4] The widespread use of Rohypnol in other countries is a major contributing factor to its abuse in the United States. According to a study published by the *Southern Medical Journal* in 2000, 8 percent of the specimens taken from 1,179 sexual assault victims nationwide tested positive for benzodiazepines.[5]

Abuse of Rohypnol in the United States was first reported in 1993 in Florida. The drug was so often seized at the U.S.-Mexican border that the Texas-Florida Rohypnol Response Group was formed in 1994 to address the problem.[6]

Due to concerns about the potential misuse of Rohypnol to aid in rape and robbery, Hoffman-Roche initiated a public relations campaign to warn of the dangers of drug-facilitated sexual assault. The company also added a dye to each tablet that releases a blue color when it is put in a liquid. In the case of Hakki, the woman who was convicted of drugging men to rob them, she overcame the obstacle of the blue dye by placing Rohypnol in red wine to mask the color. Apparently it worked, because none of the men she drugged and robbed were tipped off by a bluish tint to the wine.

Rohypnol is also popular as a recreational drug for the euphoric side effects. The use of Rohypnol recreationally is also linked with women who have a low self-esteem as it supposedly helps them escape negative feelings. Taking Rohypnol puts these women at risk for pregnancy and sexually transmitted diseases due to the higher chance of passing out or having unprotected sex.

GHB: GAMMA HYDROXYBUTYRATE

GHB, also called liquid ecstasy, easy lay, Somatomax, grievous bodily harm, and other nicknames, has a powerful sedative effect that causes amnesia, sleep, and unconsciousness. GHB can also increase secretions of growth hormone. GHB is used as a date rape drug, for muscle growth enhancement, and as a club drug because of its euphoric effects. GHB costs approximately $10 to $20 per capful (about 1 teaspoonful), which is the typical dose used to cause intoxication. It is quickly eliminated from the body, which increases its popularity with date rapists and drug users. GHB is eliminated from urine after approximately 12 hours and from blood after five hours.

Unlike Rohypnol, GHB occurs naturally in the body. GHB is a **central nervous system depressant**. Central nervous system (CNS) depressants are drugs that can slow down mental or physical functions. One of the most common CNS depressants is alcohol. Conversely, there are drugs known as **central nervous system stimulants** that speed up mental and physical functions. One common CNS stimulant is caffeine. Any drugs that speed up or slow down the central nervous system can damage the body if not taken at the appropriate levels. Even at the prescribed levels, drugs that affect the central nervous system often have side effects such as increasing blood pressure, in the case of CNS stimulants, or decreasing blood pressure, in the case of CNS depressants.

GHB toxicity has symptoms similar to Rohypnol but GHB has a higher incidence of **drop attacks**. Drop attacks are when the user suddenly loses muscle control and drops to the floor. A person experiencing a drop attack might actually still be conscious, but because of the loss of muscle control, they are at risk for being a victim of sexual assault or burglary. People who take GHB

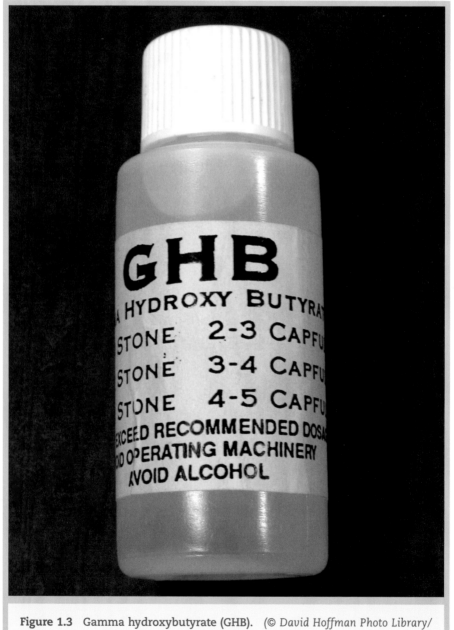

Figure 1.3 Gamma hydroxybutyrate (GHB). *(© David Hoffman Photo Library/ Alamy)*

also experience **neck snaps**. In a neck snap, the head snaps forward, which can result in injury. Some GHB users have reported becoming momentarily paralyzed to the extent that the only action they can physically control is blinking. As a central nervous system depressant, GHB relaxes muscles to the extent that users can lose control of their body. Vomiting is also associated with GHB toxicity, more so than Rohypnol or ketamine, but the reason why is unknown. The effects of GHB in the body can vary widely from one person to another.

GHB is a drug that has a narrow therapeutic window, which means that it is easy to overdose with it. At an oral dose of 25 milligrams per kilogram (mg/kg) of body weight, GHB will initiate deep sleep. At an oral dose of 60 mg/kg of body weight, GHB can induce a coma.[7] Once a person has entered a comatose state from taking GHB, the prognosis is grim. There is some indication that administering physostigmine, a drug used to treat Alzheimer's disease and glaucoma, will reverse some of the effects of GHB. According to the Centers for Disease Control (CDC), there were 69 reports of GHB-related comas in Texas and New York, with at least 10 of those people dying due to respiratory failure.

Unlike ketamine and Rohypnol, GHB is particularly difficult to control because of the presence of **analogs: gamma butyrolactone (GBL)**, and 1,4-Butanediol (1,4-BD or BD). Analogs are drugs that that have structural chemical similarity but do not necessarily have the same biological effect. In the case of GBL and 1,4-BD, these drugs have a biological effect similar to GHB and therefore both drugs pose a threat to one's health.

GBL AND BD

GBL and BD are two common drugs that are converted into GHB in the body. When they are converted, users experience relaxation and euphoria. GBL and BD are just as dangerous to human health as GHB is. Both of these compounds are prohibited from sale for human consumption; however, they are legally sold, ostensibly for industrial uses.

GBL is used in industry as a **solvent**, such as stain remover, paint stripper, and superglue remover. A solvent is a product than can mix with and dissolve another liquid, gas, or solid. Nail polish remover would be considered a solvent because it dissolves nail polish. BD is also a solvent and is used in the manufacture of plastics. BD can also be used to make GBL, which can then be used to make GHB. Solvents are very useful in the manufacturing industry but can be quite dangerous to work with because of their ability to dissolve any solids, liquids, and gases. Ingesting a solvent presents considerable health threats.

GBL is a banned chemical in the United States, Canada, and Sweden. GBL was once available as a dietary supplement, marketed to bodybuilders and also as an antiaging supplement. These products were labeled with exaggerated and unsubstantiated claims to build muscles, improve physical performance, enhance sex, reduce stress, restore youth, and induce sleep. The products were illegally marketed with unapproved drugs. Dietary supplements do not have to be approved by the U.S. Food and Drug Administration (FDA) before they are made available to the public. Only after dietary supplements have put the public's health at risk can the FDA intervene.

Some of the supplements that contained GBL were RenewTrient, Blue Nitro, Soma Solution, and Revivarent. Selling products with GBL is no longer legal, but many of the previously named dietary supplements are still sold with alternative ingredients instead of GBL. Products containing GBL or BD for consumption are still sold, either under the counter (illegally) or as an industrial product. Often these products contain ridiculous labeling such as "Warning: Accidental ingestion may cause . . . euphoria . . . increases tactile sensitivity." These products are meant to be consumed, yet the manufacturers claim they are for industrial uses. Such maneuvers to outwit the Drug Enforcement Administration (DEA) and FDA are readily apparent.

Another option for those seeking GHB or analogs is to purchase a dietary supplement from a country that has not yet outlawed GBL or BD. Americans can still illegally purchase GBL- and BD-containing substances through the Internet, particularly sites that are based in another country. Many Web hosting sites are based in the United States. The FDA and DEA will work with the Web hosting company to cease hosting a site that sells products that are harmful and illegal in the United States.

All the Web sites that sell these products boast that their product is safe and advertise GBL as a "natural" form of GHB. There is little natural about an industrial solvent such as GBL. Once the user has taken the GBL, it turns into GHB very quickly in the body. The FDA has warned about the use of GBL in dietary supplements. GBL has been linked to deaths, just as GHB has.

GHB, GBL, and BD are inexpensive and easy to synthesize. The chemicals necessary to make GHB can be purchased from numerous chemical supply houses, and recipes are easy to find. Some Web sites erroneously assure users that GHB is safe and compare the process of making GHB to brewing beer during the days of Prohibition. Many Web sites further state that GHB is legal in all countries except the United States, and point out that until recently in the United States GHB was an approved narcolepsy drug.

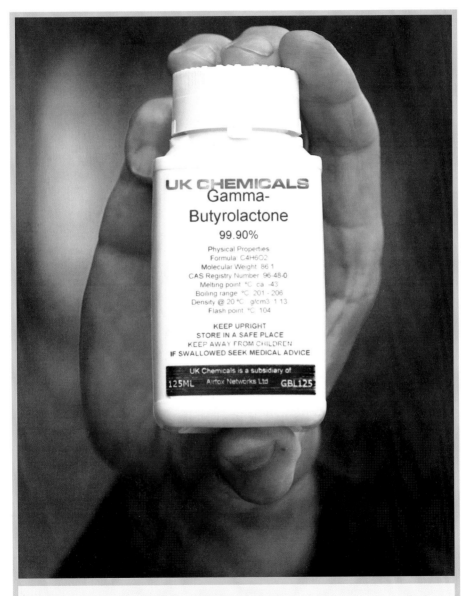

Figure 1.4 Gamma butyrolactone (GBL), a precursor of gamma hydroxybutyrate (GHB).   (© AP Images)

Taking GHB is dangerous but cooking it presents additional dangers. Preparing GHB in a kitchen poses the risk of fire and explosion from the compounds used. GBL is a solvent and can react near a flame, causing an explosion. Even if GBL is not directly placed near a flame, it can evaporate, yet still be present in the air. If this is the case, it can ignite from a spark generated by a wall switch or kitchen blender. In addition, because it is such a powerful solvent, dropping a bottle of GBL could have considerable repercussions.

Kits sold on the Internet are a popular and dangerous source of GHB. Between 1999 and 2000, two brothers from Mississippi and South Carolina sold GHB kits over the Internet for $55. Each kit, which contained GBL and sodium hydroxide, could make 15 to 20 doses. Sodium hydroxide is needed to turn GBL into GHB, although as explained above, merely consuming GBL causes the compound to metabolize in the body. The brothers disguised their kits as computer-cleaning solvents, evidently thinking this would be enough to stay under the DEA's radar. The New Jersey Statewide Narcotics Task Force went undercover and purchased nine kits via the Web site, and New Jersey police seized a 55-gallon drum of GBL and 10 pounds of sodium hydroxide from one brother's home in South Carolina. In 2002 the brothers pleaded guilty and were sentenced to four years in prison.[8]

According to the FDA, GBL-related products have been associated with at least 55 adverse health events in the United States, including one death. In 19 cases the individuals became unconscious or comatose, and several required intubation for assisted breathing. Other reported effects included seizures, vomiting, slow breathing, and slow heart rate. There have been reports of at least five children under 18 years of age who have been injured or who have suffered these kinds of effects.[9]

GBL has been responsible for deaths in other countries. In England in 2009, Hester Stewart was partying with friends following an awards ceremony and consumed the liquid form of GBL along with a small amount of alcohol, based on toxicology results. Stewart died that evening. It is unclear whether Stewart knowingly took the drug or it was slipped into her alcoholic beverage. Her friends claimed she would never take drugs. Stewart, who aspired to become a surgeon, was at the top of her class studying molecular medicine at Sussex University. She was paid by the university to act as a mentor to first-year students. Stewart died at age 21.

Sadly, England had promised in 2008, just one year before Stewart's death, to ban GBL but had failed to institute such a ban. GBL is cheap and easily obtained on the Internet. Because it is not banned in England, it is perfectly legal to possess, distribute, and consume GBL in England. In the United States, GBL is illegal to possess for human consumption.

A male friend claimed he took the drug with Stewart. He was not charged with anything since his actions were not illegal. GHB, however, has been banned in England since 2003. Stewart was the third person in 2009 to have died from taking GBL, which is becoming more popular in England's club scene.

GHB AS A DATE RAPE DRUG

GHB is used to facilitate date rape because it reduces the will to resist, relaxes muscles, and causes disinhibition and amnesia. GHB also supposedly increases the desire for sex. In a 2000 study published in the *Southern Medical Journal,* a higher percentage of 1,179 sexual assault victims tested positive for GHB than Rohypnol.[10] Also detected in victims' samples were GBL and BD. When consumed, BD takes effect in five to 20 minutes and lasts two to three hours.

GHB AND ATHLETIC PERFORMANCE

GHB is used by many people, almost exclusively men, to increase muscle mass. GHB stimulates the release of growth hormone and prolactin. **Prolactin** is a hormone that is associated with the production of milk in the body (lactation). In the 1980s GHB was promoted as a body-building aid in supplements. By the late 1980s GHB became labeled as a drug of abuse by those looking to enhance their athletic performance or to build muscle. Since GHB is highly damaging and addictive to the body, there is little valid scientific information on the ability of GHB to develop muscle. GHB in dietary supplements was banned in the United States due to its potential for abuse.

GHB AS A CLUB DRUG

Joe is a 35-year-old footwear designer who lives, works, and parties in New York City. Joe is single with a wide network of successful friends. Joe considers himself fit and healthy. He works out at the gym religiously and never eats fast food. If it could be said that Joe has any bad habits, it would be the occasional use of GHB at clubs. Joe does not take GHB every weekend, nor does he ever crave it. He has never bought it. If it is offered to him, however, he cannot resist.

Joe gets GHB from a well-trusted friend. Joe is not concerned about the safety of GHB since he has heard it is a natural substance that is found in the body. Out of curiosity, Joe asked his friend where he got it, since he knew it was illegal. Joe's friend said he purchased it over the Internet. The friend said it was sold as a kit and he had to mix the chemicals himself. The idea of his friend, who works as a massage therapist, acting like a chemist makes Joe a little uneasy, but all his other friends take GHB without any

THE DANGERS OF RAVES

Raves are parties characterized by rapidly pounding, loud music, in dark, crowded, and often unlicensed venues such as warehouses, private homes, or even outside. Ravers wave glow sticks in the darkness to enhance the hallucinogenic effects of the drugs they take while dancing. Fog, fire, and videos can also be part of the rave experience.

Raves became popular in England in the 1970s and then expanded their popularity to the United States by the late 1980s. By the 1990s raves were widespread and were viewed as a subculture due to the use of drugs and secrecy (raves usually moved from location to location, sometimes on short notice). The appeal of raves to some people, particularly those underage, was the prevalence of drugs and lack of supervision. GHB, ketamine, and Rohypnol, as well as Ecstasy (MDMA) are all known to be used at raves. The sedative and hallucinogenic effect of these drugs appeals to ravers. Ketamine distorts perceptions of sight and sound, making the drug complement the atmosphere of swirling lights, gyrating bodies, and pulsing music. In addition, GHB, ketamine, and Rohypnol are relatively inexpensive, therefore increasingly accessible. Now, raves are not as common as they were in the 1990s due to police intervention because of reports of drug use and concerns over large groups of people gathering in places not licensed for dancing, amplified music, or large crowds.

serious side effects. Once he takes the drug, he usually never gives it another thought.

Joe takes GHB in liquid form, doled out in the cap of a soda bottle at the club. Joe always pours his capful of GHB in his drink because otherwise it has a strong salty flavor and unappealing odor. Joe has noticed a wide variability in how even one capful of GHB affects him. He isn't sure if that has something to do with his own body chemistry, other supplements he might have taken that day, or the result of his friend inadvertently altering the potency by mixing it himself. After a few experiments with GHB, Joe quickly learned that there was a fine line between GHB relaxing him to a comfortable state of euphoria and making him feel so sleepy that he could barely keep his eyes open. One of the things Joe liked about GHB was that it never gave him a hangover the next day and usually, within a few hours, whatever effect GHB had on him, it seemed to be out of his system.

In most of the instances when Joe took GHB, he felt an increase in his sex drive and even ended up in bed at the end of the night with people he never previously felt attracted to. When Joe was with someone while on GHB, even kissing seemed much more intense, as if the GHB heightened all of his senses. Joe was well educated about the dangers of unprotected sex. He was particularly wary of the combination of increased sexual desire from GHB and decreased inhibitions. This combination had led many of his friends to have unprotected sex while high. He knew of one friend who contracted HIV and blamed it on an evening of unprotected sex while on GHB with someone he had met at the club.

Joe knew to be cautious with GHB because he had heard stories of "friends of friends" who had taken too much and ended up having a seizure or going to the hospital. He had even heard of one person who was addicted to GHB dying in a fire. The addict passed out after a night of heavy GHB use while smoking in bed. Those are people that are addicted to GHB, Joe always thought, and Joe felt grateful that he considered himself well in control of his GHB usage.

Joe's perception of GHB mirrors many of those who use GHB. GHB is in fact very dangerous to use recreationally because of its toxicity and potential for abuse and addiction. GHB has a narrow therapeutic window, which means that the range between feeling GHB's effect and overdosing on it is relatively small. People who take GHB risk seizure, coma, and death. In addition, taking drugs or alcohol increases sedation, which puts the user at greater risk for overdosing. It is easier for a voluntary user of GHB to become a victim of sexual assault, because many might pass out and then be taken advantage of. In one survey on the use of recreational GHB, one respondent said that he passed out and then when he awoke, a person was having unprotected sex with him.[11]

GHB AND NARCOLEPSY

Narcolepsy is an extremely rare disease, occurring in only 0.05 percent of the population. This percentage equates to approximately 140,000 people in the United States who suffer from narcolepsy.[12] Narcolepsy is a disorder most notable for attacks that cause sudden sleep even in the middle of a conversation. Narcoleptics experience severe daytime sleepiness even when they have had a full night of sleep. The extent of this daytime sleepiness is comparable to having foregone sleep for two or three days.

Narcoleptics also have irregular nighttime sleep. A normal sleep pattern involves a critical process known as rapid eye movement (REM), where brain activity picks up after about an hour or two of slower brain waves, and dreams occur as well as eye movement. A lack of muscle tone also occurs during **REM sleep**. Narcoleptics fall into REM sleep as soon as they fall asleep. Narcoleptics also fall into REM during the day.

Narcoleptics also often suffer from **cataplexy**. Cataplexy is the sudden weakness of muscle control triggered by laughter, anger, embarrassment, surprise, or any other sudden emotion or event. The backfire of a car can jolt a narcoleptic into cataplexy.

Fortunately, GHB has been beneficial for the treatment of narcolepsy and cataplexy. In the 1970s doctors began to administer GHB to narcoleptics after scientists discovered that GHB-induced anesthesia resembled natural sleep in terms of periods of REM. In 2002 the FDA approved **Xyrem** (sodium oxybate) to treat excessive daytime sleepiness and cataplexy. In 2002 Xyrem was made available to an estimated 140,000 narcoleptics in the United States.[13]

The approval of GHB to treat narcoleptics was highly controversial due to the drug's potential for diversion for date rape or other illicit uses. The resolution was the approval of Xyrem under a very strict distribution program, named the Xyrem Patient Success Program. The exact way in which Xyrem helps to treat narcolepsy, referred to as a drug's **mechanism of action**, is unknown. This might seem unusual, but there are many FDA-approved drugs that have an unknown mechanism of action. Xyrem is a central nervous system depressant that makes a person very drowsy. Xyrem is taken by narcoleptics at night, preferably when they are in bed. Food can affect the efficacy of Xyrem and therefore narcoleptics must be sure to eat dinner several hours before they take their first nightly dose of Xyrem.

Doses are prepared by combining Xyrem in two ounces of water. The narcoleptic must then set an alarm to wake up again two and a half to four hours after the first dose to take the second dose of Xyrem. Since Xyrem is a central nervous system depressant, taking the full dose at the beginning of the night might cause the person to have respiratory failure, become unconscious, or have a seizure. Narcoleptics who choose to take Xyrem must adhere to a strict schedule of taking the drug and agree not to use alcohol or any other sedatives while on Xyrem. Sedatives and alcohol are depressants, as is Xyrem, and to combine depressants presents a risk to health. Although having to wake up to take medication and adhering to a specific schedule of eating and bedtime might seem like a hassle, the narcoleptic's quality of life is greatly improved.

KETAMINE

Ketamine (pronounced kee-ta-meen) is a white powder that was approved in the United States for use as an anesthetic for humans and animals in 1970. Ketamine is a powerful anesthetic and **analgesic** (painkiller) that can cause amnesia and hallucinations. Ketamine also functions as a fast-acting antidepressant taking effect within a few hours instead of a week or longer as is typical with other currently available antidepressants. One subanaesthetic dose of ketamine can sustain an antidepressant effect for up to a week and might provide an alternative to patients who have not had success with traditional antidepressants.[14]

Today ketamine is a controlled but legal drug, although its use is relatively limited in the United States. At this time, ketamine is not FDA-approved for the treatment of depression. Ketamine, however, is still considered a medically valuable drug and is listed as a core medicine in the World Health Organization's "Essential Drug List." This list includes drugs the World Health Organization has judged to be necessary for a country's basic health care system.

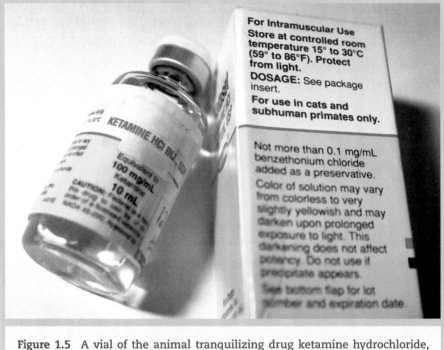

Figure 1.5 A vial of the animal tranquilizing drug ketamine hydrochloride, better known in the drug culture as "Special K." (© *AP Images*)

Ketamine replaced PCP (phencyclidine), which was developed in 1950 as an anesthetic. PCP was discontinued in 1965 primarily because of the side effects of agitation, paranoia, and delusions. Approximately 90 percent of the ketamine sold legally today is for veterinary use as a tranquilizer. Some veterinary clinics have been robbed by those seeking "Vitamin K" as a club or rape drug. A very small percentage of ketamine is used on humans for pediatric and obstetric procedures as a painkiller.

Ketamine is classified as a dissociative anesthetic, just as PCP is, and it can leave users in a stupor for hours. A dissociative anesthetic is one that blocks signals in the brain to the conscious mind and produces a feeling of detachment from pain. In the case of ketamine and PCP, the result can cause hallucinations and even euphoria. According to one ketamine user, "If you take enough ketamine, it will give you a preview of your own death, put you in contact with seraph-like entities, and convince you that you've just seen God in a disco ball."[15]

When used legitimately, ketamine is injected intravenously. In the illegal market, ketamine is often formulated into a powder, as a result of evaporating it from the liquid form, and then snorted, although it can be irritating to the nose. In some cases, users will inject it, which creates a more rapid high that occurs within 30 seconds. Snorted, ketamine usually takes effect in five to 10 minutes. An oral dose is the slowest, with an effect that takes place in 10 to 30 minutes on an empty stomach.

Users of ketamine refer to it as the perfect "escape drug" because it has the ability to bring a person into a whole other world with heavy use, referred to as a K-trip. Ketamine is often taken with other drugs—a practice known as **polydrugging**—such as marijuana and ecstasy (MDMA). Ketamine can cause unconsciousness, permanent brain damage, and death, even when it is not combined with alcohol or another drug. The Drug Abuse Warning Network (DAWN), a national drug abuse surveillance system that monitors emergency room visits and deaths attributable to drug abuse, documented at least two ketamine-related deaths between 1993 and 1997 in which no other drugs, including alcohol, were used.

HONG KONG'S DRUG OF CHOICE

After spending the day in Victoria Bay, one of the largest harbors in the world, Marilee was looking forward to getting a taste of night life in Hong Kong's Central District. The Central District was throbbing with people, even more crowded than the New York City bars. Inside the clubs were swirling lights and provocatively dressed women urging men to come inside. At one point, Marilee was approached by a couple of good-looking young Hong Kong men to dance. Marilee and her friends danced and chatted with the men and were having a good time despite the slight language barrier. Marilee was surprised when one of the guys pulled out a small piece of paper with a tiny white crystal in it. The guy put his arm around her and said it was his treat, it would make her feel happy, nothing more. Marilee slipped out of his embrace and whispered to her friends that they should move on. Marilee did not believe in taking drugs, particularly one from a stranger in another country. Luckily for Marilee, she made the right choice.

In Hong Kong ketamine has become a popular drug among young people. Ketamine is relatively cheap and available when compared with other

BURGLARY AND DATE RAPE DRUGS

Burglary is another motivation for slipping a date rape drug into a person's drink. In Germany it was reported that **methylprylone** was used by prostitutes in St. Pauli, the "red light" district of Hamburg, to drug and subsequently rob their clients. Methylprylone is a sedative in the piperidinedione family of drugs and has been replaced by better-performing benzodiazepines (discussed later in this book).

In 2004, 37-year-old Selina Hakki was convicted of drugging wealthy men she met at exclusive London nightspots with Rohyphol and then robbing them. In one case Hakki stole Versace clothes, three Rolex watches, shoes, and a Tiffany clock. Hakki was the first woman to be convicted of such a crime, and she was sentenced to five years in prison.

In a subsequent case a 40-year-old bar owner told two women, ages 23 and 25, that they could stay at his apartment after they told him that they missed the last bus home. The three purchased a bottle of champagne at a convenience store before they arrived at his apartment, where they drank together. The next morning the bar owner woke up naked without any recollection of anything after he drank the champagne. All items of value were gone from the apartment, as were the two women.

The bar owner reported the event to the police. His blood and urine samples tested positive for Rohypnol. The man could provide only a vague description of the women, but surveillance video from the convenience store provided enough video to identify them. When questioned by police, the women admitted to dissolving five tablets of Rohypnol in a small bottle of water at home. They then mixed this solution with the man's champagne.[16]

narcotics in Hong Kong. One gram of ketamine in Hong Kong sells for the equivalent of $13 and is enough for two people to get high; whereas cocaine sells for the equivalent of $103 a gram. Ketamine is legal for medical use in Hong Kong and is produced as a clear liquid that can be evaporated into a white crystal. It is through this crystalline form that ketamine is often sold on the streets, usually wrapped in a small piece of paper. Often, though, the drug is **trafficked** from other parts of Asia such as India and China.

KETAMINE AND THE BRAIN

Since ketamine alters brain signaling and can cause hallucinations, long-term use can affect **cognitive functioning**. Cognitive functioning enables a person to reason and use judgment, and is the source of awareness and proper perception. Similar to many drugs, ketamine can damage internal organs, such as the liver. Drugs are usually metabolized in the liver. The liver essentially breaks down the drug into smaller compounds to be flushed out of the body. Consistent use of any drug, even if it is taken in prescribed doses, risks damaging the liver. Taken in high doses, ketamine can be fatal. Forty-six ketamine-related deaths were reported between 1994 and 1998, according to DAWN.

The prevalence of ketamine abuse from users seeking a high is relatively low when compared to other drugs. According to The Partnership for a Drug-Free America's 2009 report, the prevalence of users in grade 8 was 1.2 percent and the prevalence of users in grade 12 was 1.5 percent.

2
Historical Use of GHB, Ketamine, and Rohypnol

GHB, ketamine, and Rohypnol were originally developed to alleviate pain and anxiety, specifically as an anesthetic, sedative, or both. The creators of these medications most certainly did not intend that these drugs would be used to facilitate crimes or voluntarily consumed without medical necessity by healthy individuals.

Often, however, the path that a drug will take has less to do with the intentions of a drug company or the scientists who are part of the discovery of the drug but how a drug is received by the public. Favorability or the unpleasantness of side effects will have a considerable impact on a drug's use and misuse. As a result, the unintended uses of a drug will shape the regulations, scheduling, and possible distribution of the drug. In the cases of GHB, ketamine, and Rohypnol, their reception in the marketplace and the availability of alternatives has sculpted each drug's history.

THE DISCOVERY OF GHB

In 1961 Dr. Henri Laborit, a French researcher, was first to create GHB in a lab. Laborit was a neurosurgeon in the marines and became interested in GHB for its role in reducing shock to injured military personnel. Laborit knew that GHB increased dopamine. He observed that drugs that increase dopamine generally had the effect of reducing a patient's awareness of his surroundings and easing shock.

When Laborit created GHB, it was not known that GHB occurs naturally in the body. In 1963 GHB was discovered to exist in the brain. In the 1970s GHB was first prescribed as a treatment for insomnia and for narcolepsy.

Figure 2.1 In 1961 Dr. Henri Laborit, a French researcher, was first to create GHB in a lab. *(National Library of Medicine)*

GHB AS A SUPPLEMENT IN THE 1980s

GHB was promoted as a supplement in health food stores because it was believed to improve athletic performance, reduce stress, and burn fat. After people started taking GHB, users reported having difficulty breathing, vomiting, and seizures. In rare cases coma and even death were associated with GHB. In the late 1980s GHB became known as a drug of abuse.

Gamma butyrolactone (GBL) is a precursor to GHB. A precursor is a chemical that changes into another drug, for example, if GBL is combined with the appropriate chemical, it will become GHB. The chemical 1,4-butanediol (also known as BD) is a precursor to GBL. GBL is a chemical found in nail polish, glue removers, and floor cleaners. The significance of these precursors is that they are all readily available, thus making GHB much easier to make and use illegally.

GHB and all of the precursors increase the effects of alcohol and are even more dangerous when taken along with other drugs. In 1990, after approximately 30 GHB-related illnesses, the FDA banned it in supplements. GHB is currently banned in the United States and England but is still obtained illegally. Since GHB is illegal, users will use precursors to GHB: GBL and BD are converted to GHB in the body. GBL and BD are not approved for human consumption by the FDA but they exist because the chemicals are used to make floor stripper, paint thinner, and other industrial products.

GHB IN THE 1990s: THE CLUB DRUG

GHB is also known as liquid Ecstasy because of its sedative and euphoric effects. GHB becomes particularly powerful in club settings because it is often combined with alcohol. Both alcohol and GHB are central nervous system depressants, and taking both drugs has an **additive effect**: the effect of the alcohol and the effect of the GHB equal the sum of the depressant effects of each of the drugs. An additive effect is also explained as $1 + 1 = 2$, instead of the effect of one drug increasing the effect of the second drug.

People who take GHB recreationally generally do so because of the euphoric and relaxing effects, as well as increasing the drive for sex. Combining a carefree spirit and an increased drive for sex presents a greater potential for sexually transmitted diseases and unwanted pregnancy.

GHB TO TREAT ALCOHOLISM

Alcoholism is a chronic disease in which the individual craves alcohol both physically and psychologically. Alcoholism is detrimental to the alcoholic's personal and professional life. If left untreated, alcoholism is often fatal. Alcoholics can die indirectly, such as through drinking and driving, or from organ failure, particularly liver failure.

Withdrawing from alcohol is a very uncomfortable experience for an alcoholic. Depending on their degree of chemical dependence, going "cold turkey" can even be life threatening. Some of the symptoms include nausea, vomiting, shaking, irritability, headache, anxiety, and an increase in heart rate and blood pressure. People who withdraw from alcohol describe the feeling as an intense hangover even if they did not drink the night before. Perhaps most difficult is that the individual will experience intense cravings for alcohol. The knowledge that consuming alcohol will make symptoms go away makes it particularly difficult for those recovering to stay on track.

To improve an alcoholic's chance of resisting alcohol, GHB can be helpful to ease symptoms and reduce long-term cravings. In one experiment, two groups of alcoholics who had stopped consumption of all alcohol were compared for the following factors: tremors, sweating, nausea, depression, anxiety, and restlessness. One group was given a dose of GHB in strong-tasting cherry syrup and the other group was given the strong-tasting cherry syrup without any GHB or any other drug in it. (The group that does not receive the drug is referred to as the **control group**.) The participants were not told, nor were the professionals administering the two types of syrups told, which group received the concoction containing GHB. This type of experiment, in which neither the participant nor the person administering the dose is privy to who is receiving the drug, is known as a **double blind experiment**. A double blind experiment helps prevent bias in an experiment because neither the patient nor person giving the drug knows who is in the control group and who is in the test group.

Medical professionals monitored the blood pressure and heart rates of both groups. Control patients continued to receive non-GHB treatment for their alcoholism but the test group continued to receive GHB three times a day at a dose based on their body weight. According to the 1989 study that was published in the medical journal *The Lancet*, the group receiving GHB

fared much better—the severity of their withdrawal symptoms decreased dramatically within one hour of receiving their first dose of GHB. Test group participants continued to have a lessening of withdrawal symptoms for eight hours after they received GHB, whereas the control group suffered increasing withdrawal symptoms. After three days, the test group had their GHB reduced by 30 percent, and it was discontinued on the eighth day. Unfortunately, the study did not provide follow-up data.[1]

Even alcoholics who have successfully withdrawn from alcohol will continue to have cravings throughout their life. GHB has been shown to also help with these long-term cravings. In one experiment, recovering alcoholics were given small doses of GHB three times a day. The majority of people in this group, 66 percent, indicated lower desires to drink as compared to only 25 percent of the recovering alcoholics in the control group.

GHB TO EASE HEROIN WITHDRAWAL

Heroin is an opiate, derived from the opium poppy. Typical of most drugs in the opiate family, heroin causes a rush of euphoria, particularly when injected because of the quick absorption into the body. Heroin is addictive both physically and psychologically with withdrawal symptoms that are unpleasant enough to cause relapse just to seek the release from withdrawal symptoms.

Jackie, 27, was a heroin addict who tried to kick her habit numerous times. Each time she tried to stop taking heroin she experienced nausea, cramping, headaches, sweating, watery eyes and nose, sensitivity to light and pain, weakness, insomnia, and of course an overwhelming craving for heroin. Jackie had been addicted to heroin for four years and her habit had grown to nearly 2 grams daily. In the Unites States, 1 gram of heroin costs approximately $300 depending on purity.

Jackie had not lived at home for eight years but was still in touch with her family. Witnessing Jackie's rapid decline and fearing for her life, they approached her about her addiction and offered her help. Jackie welcomed their assistance.

Jackie's father had read a scientific paper published in an international journal of neuropsychiatry by Italian researchers who had used GHB to mitigate the effects of heroin withdrawal. Jackie's father was willing to try anything, and was willing to give GHB a try since he knew how horribly his daughter suffered from trying to kick her heroin habit. Jackie agreed to move home with her parents so they could administer the GHB and monitor her. Jackie's father gave her GHB in a dose determined by her body weight (0.025 g of GHB per kg of body weight) every three to four hours during the acute withdrawal phase, which is usually the first three or four days. Jackie's father was sure to administer a dose just before bedtime so that she would have a better chance of sleeping through the night. If Jackie awoke during the night, he administered another dose while she was awake.

Keeping in mind the sedating effects of GHB alone, Jackie's father was sure to be with his daughter at all times so that he could assist her with getting up and walking around if she needed to use the bathroom. GHB alone is very sedating, so it was expected that without a caretaker Jackie would be groggy and more likely to hurt herself by falling.

After a few days of her GHB treatment and cessation of heroin, Jackie told her father that GHB was nothing short of a miracle for her. Jackie felt that GHB reduced her withdrawal symptoms to one-tenth of what they had been in the past without GHB. GHB enabled Jackie to accomplish what she had tried repeatedly in the past: stop using heroin.[2]

ROHYPNOL: A SLEEP AID, THEN AND NOW

Flunitrazepam, the drug contained in Rohypnol, was first approved for use in the 1960s by Hoffman-LaRoche, Inc. It was later marketed as Rohypnol in Switzerland in 1975. Flunitrazepam has never been legal in the United States because safer drugs exist to treat insomnia and as a preoperative anesthetic.

Flunitrazepam is commonly prescribed in Europe for elderly insomniacs. As a person ages, high quality sleep becomes more difficult to achieve. The disadvantage of taking flunitrazepam is that although the insomniac is able to fall asleep, she or he usually feels groggy upon awakening, described by users as akin to a hangover. Despite these side effects, many European insomniacs still choose to take flunitrazepam to fall asleep at night.

Flunitrazepam began being abused in Europe in the late 1970s. Even though it was never legal in the United States, flunitrazepam was illegally imported into the United States, primarily to Texas and Florida, in the late 1980s where it was used as a recreational drug by college and high school students.

In an attempt to more tightly regulate Rohypnol, the World Health Organization changed the drug's status from Schedule IV to Schedule III. Tighter drug regulations help to minimize abuse. but as long as Rohypnol is legal in other countries, keeping it out of the United States is impossible. In many other countries, Rohypnol can be purchased over the counter for the treatment of insomnia.

KETAMINE: REPLACING PCP

In 1962 ketamine was created by scientists who were searching for a replacement for PCP as an anaesthetic. Ketamine was marketed under the trade name Ketalar by Parke-Davis. PCP had been used an anesthetic since 1958 but had a high incidence of causing hallucinations, delirium, and psychotic reactions. Ketamine seemed superior to PCP as an aesthetic since it did not appear to cause hallucinations at the doses used as anesthesia. Ketamine had a minimal effect on the respiratory and cardiac systems and did not significantly suppress breathing. If used for surgery, ketamine also wears off quickly after a procedure. Currently, ketamine is sold as a generic prescription drug in Europe for general anesthesia.

Ketamine began gaining popularity in the 1970s along with the New Age movement. One leader of the movement, Dr. John Lilly, advocated the use of ketamine to achieve a so-called higher level of consciousness. Dr. John Lilly was a physician, writer, and philosopher who believed in the use of psychedelic drugs such as ketamine and LSD to "enlighten" oneself. Dr. Lilly also wrote extensively on the topics of dolphin communication and the isolation tank. Lilly wrote *The Scientist: A Metaphysical Autobiography* in 1978 and created a following that increased the use of ketamine recreationally. *The Scientist* is still available and being read today. Many believe Lilly was ahead of his time in writing about altering states of consciousness. As long as there are scientists who advocate using drugs, so too will there be people who take drugs based solely on the advice of someone they perceive as an authority.

In the 1980s ketamine became a popular recreational drug because consumption of large doses caused sensations and hallucinations similar to those associated with PCP. People who used ketamine in this way were far different than the followers of Dr. John Lilly. These people were interested not in self-discovery but in enhancing the party experience via the euphoric rush and out-of-body experience that ketamine offers.

Since the 1980s the illegal use and distribution of ketamine has been a concern of the FDA, DEA, and U.S. Department of Health and Human Services (DHHS). In 1981 the DEA became concerned about the use of ketamine as a recreational drug and subsequently made a request to DHHS to evaluate ketamine medically and recommend a scheduling classification. Because ketamine has legitimate uses, a complete ban is not likely. The DEA again in 1986 and 1998 asked DHHS to make a medical and scientific evaluation of ketamine in the hope of getting the FDA to put ketamine in the more restrictive Schedule III. Today ketamine is a Schedule III drug, although many drug awareness advocates believe that a Schedule II classification would help control the illegal distribution of ketamine.

KETAMINE THERAPY FOR HEROIN ADDICTS

Heroin addicts face unpleasant withdrawal symptoms. Nausea, vomiting, diarrhea, chills, sweating, tears, difficulty sleeping, aches and pains in the muscles and joints, extreme restlessness, and dilated pupils are just some of what they will experience within the first three days after their last dose. It is during this time that the craving for heroin is the strongest.

Recovering addicts also experience psychological symptoms, including anxiety and depression. Ketamine has been used to encourage abstinence from heroin. A high dose of ketamine has a better chance of keeping a former heroin addict clean than does a low dose. This treatment is called ketamine psychotherapy. Typically, **psychotherapy** includes sessions with a therapist to treat psychological and emotional disorders. Ketamine psychotherapy adds doses of ketamine to the patient treatment regimen.

An experiment was performed at the St. Petersburg Research Center of Addictions and Psychopharmacology in Russia, and results were published in 2002. Seventy detoxified heroin-addicted patients were in one of two groups that received two different doses of ketamine. One group received psychotherapy in addition to a dose of ketamine large enough to cause hallucinations. The patients in the other group received the same psychotherapy but a lower dose of ketamine that would not cause hallucinations. Neither

(*continues on page 40*)

COUNTERFEIT DRUGS AND THE INTERNET

Many people today feel comfortable making purchases over the Internet, including prescription drugs. It could even be argued that the Internet serves as a pharmacy that can ship products globally. With new Internet drug vendors popping up frequently, the FDA has warned about the possible dangers of purchasing prescription drugs in this manner. The problem of counterfeit drugs making it into the U.S. supply of drugs is a significant and growing issue. The number of counterfeit-drug investigations by the FDA has increased fourfold since the late 1990s and continues to be a problem.

In several cases, the FDA has discovered the sale of counterfeit drugs through these Internet-based pharmacies. Counterfeit drugs are considered fake medicine by the FDA and are illegal. These drugs may be contaminated or contain the wrong or no active ingredient and therefore can present a threat to human health.

Weight loss drugs are one of the FDA's biggest targets. In January 2010 the FDA discovered counterfeit Alli (orlistat), a weight loss drug, being sold via online auctions, such as eBay. Alli is composed of FDA-approved lipase inhibitors that can be purchased over the counter (without a prescription). Lipase inhibitors reduce the body's ability to absorb fat, generally by one-third. Alli blocks the enzyme that breaks down fat: lipase. Any fat consumed is passed through the body, which poses some undesirable side effects such as diarrhea.

The FDA discovered that fake Alli did not contain what it was supposed to: orlistat. Instead the counterfeit drug contained sibutramine, which is the active ingredient in another weight-loss drug, Meridia. Sibutramine is a stimulant drug approved by the FDA in 1997 for weight loss. This drug has been associated with increased blood pressure, headaches, dry mouth, insomnia, and constipation, and should not be taken by people who have a history of heart disease or stroke. People who take certain antidepressants that increase levels of **serotonin** cannot take sibutramine because of the risk of **serotonin toxicity.** In addition, the dosing instructions recommend users take three times the daily dose for sibutramine. This type of drug switch is particularly dangerous to people with heart problems and could be fatal.

Even people who do not have heart problems could suffer serious side effects because of the mislabeled dosing for sibutramine. These side effects include a racing heart, insomnia, anxiety, and nausea.

The fake Alli looks very similar to the real Alli with only a few differences such as an expiration date with month, day, and year on the fake Alli, whereas the real Alli only displays a month and year. There are a few other minor differences in the fake Alli that are unlikely to be detected by consumers unless they have been alerted to the distribution of the counterfeit Alli. In many cases the FDA discovers counterfeit drugs based on consumer complaints.

In 2007 the FDA received complaints that a counterfeit weight-loss drug was sold to three consumers on two different Web sites. The sites claimed to be selling Xenical, an FDA-approved drug meant for obese patients who meet specific height and weight requirements. Lab tests eventually showed that the product sold did not

(continues)

Figure 2.2 Internet pharmacies have proven difficult to regulate and can be a source of counterfeit drugs. *(© Snap!photo/iStockphoto)*

(continued)
contain any of the active ingredients found in authentic Xenical. Instead, the pills contained the active ingredient sibutramine, similar to the fake Alli.

The FDA also discovered that other samples from these Web sites contained only talc and starch, despite the fact that the packaging contained a valid lot number. A lot number indicates specifics of where the drug was manufactured. The lot number listed on the drug did not correlate, however, with the true expiration date for that lot. Instead, the expiration was listed as April 2007, whereas the real expiration date of the lot was March 2005. Further investigation revealed that these two Web sites, www.brandpills.com and www.pillspharm.com, had been implicated previously in selling counterfeit drugs that it claimed could fight avian flu. Both of these companies are based outside the United States. The FDA recommends that consumers exercise caution when buying any drugs over the Internet and be particularly wary if there is no way to contact anyone at the Web site by phone or if the drugs seem much cheaper than usual.

The Internet has vastly changed the availability of drugs and threatened the quality of the drug supply and therefore the health of Americans. The Internet is a wonderful tool for purchasing airline tickets, electronics, and many other items, but it is best to trust only local pharmacies or mail-order services with a physical address in the United States to purchase prescription medication. Even if a Web site claims to be based in Canada, the FDA has found that often the drugs are manufactured in a far-off country where far fewer drug regulations exist when compared with the United States.

(continued from page 37)
the therapist nor the patient knew which group was which (a double-blind experiment).

The therapy included preparation for the ketamine session, the ketamine session itself, and post-session psychotherapy aimed to help patients to integrate insights from their hallucinations into everyday life. Patients in the group that received the higher dose experienced a full psychedelic experience and discussed these experiences with their therapist. The therapist helped the patient integrate insights from the ketamine session into their everyday life. After two years of follow-up, the individuals who received the higher dose of ketamine had a significantly greater rate of abstinence within the first two years after the experiment than those who had therapy with the lower dose of ketamine.[3]

This type of experiment is highly controversial and differs extensively from other applications of drugs to help promote abstinence in an addict. In most cases, drugs are used to help with the physical withdrawal symptoms. In ketamine therapy, ketamine is used to help exclusively with psychological dependence of a drug.

This type of research seems to fall in line with Dr. Lilly's work wherein ketamine was part of a New Age movement to safely induce a "transpersonal state" on the assumption that this experience would have a profound healing potential. This philosophy was popular in Europe, which is why almost all the literature on ketamine psychotherapy comes from Europe. A transpersonal state is considered to be achieved when a person is aware of his or her spirit beyond their social conditioning, or what society expects of them. If one has a belief in a transpersonal state, ketamine's role as a dissociative (which occurs when users describe an out-of-body experience) seems a likely vehicle for this condition, if it really exists. By disconnecting from social conditioning, such as parental expectations, the person would therefore have a better way to learn about themselves. It is unlikely that ketamine hypnotherapy will become popular in the United States.

ABUSE OF PRESCRIPTION DRUGS

The abuse of prescription drugs is increasing and online pharmacies have only added to this trend. Many of these Internet-based pharmacies do not require a prescription even for legal drugs and are often located in countries that the United States has no control over. A quick Internet search of the keywords "GHB and purchase" reveals a Web site with the slogan, "G Monster—Buy Natural GHB," that promotes G Monster as a natural alternative to GHB. The Web site does not indicate what is contained in the alternative GHB. The Web site promotes G Monster as making a person very drowsy in 15 minutes

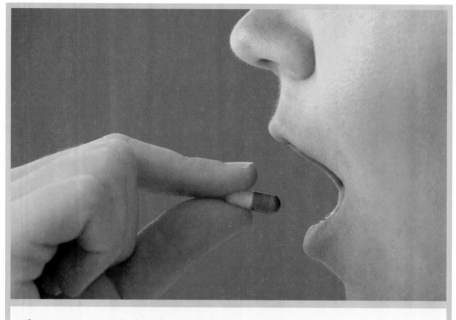

Figure 2.3 Prescription drug abuse is a growing problem in the United States. *(© tomazl/iStockphoto)*

but also cautions that results vary per person. Unfortunately it does not warn that results can also vary based on other medications a person is taking, alcohol consumption, and drug allergies.

Many Web sites proudly declare that a prescription is not required. Other Web sites require purchasers to fill out a questionnaire and state that answers will be evaluated, but often there is no proof or information about the identity or qualifications of the supposed reviewer. The safety of the questionnaire method also requires that the person is answering the questions truthfully, when in fact, the correct answers would be easy to discern. In addition to regulating the safety, effectiveness and manufacturing of pharmaceutical drugs, the FDA also regulates the prescribing process. Specifically, the sale of a prescription drug must accompany a prescription. The FDA can prohibit these Web sites that do not require a prescription from selling to any Americans, but since many of these companies are based outside of the United States, the sites are difficult to shut down entirely.

According to the International Narcotics Control Board (INCB), the level of abuse of prescription drugs—including stimulants such as methylphenidate (Ritalin) and amphetamine derivatives (Adderall) and depressants such as GHB and Rohypnol—is no less than the level of abuse of drugs such as ecstasy, cocaine, methamphetamine, and heroin. In parts of Europe, Africa, and South Asia, prescription drug abuse has escalated to the point that they are traded in larger quantities than traditional trafficked drugs such as cocaine and heroin. The unregulated markets in these countries mean it is much easier for these drugs to make it into the United States.

3
Biological Mechanisms of Date Rape Drugs

Mary was a 22-year-old college student who went to a local bar with her friends. During a Saturday evening she consumed two alcoholic drinks in a five-hour period, which was normal for her once a week. She was with a large group of friends and did not worry about mingling with strangers.

While on the crowded and dark dance floor, a tall man with long dark hair leaned in to her very closely. Soon after speaking with this man she felt lightheaded and heavily intoxicated. She also felt extremely tired and felt herself falling asleep as the man was talking to her. He escorted her to a bar stool and then suggested that he drive her home.

The rest of the evening was a blur to her but her friends told her that the tall man with the long dark hair had one hand on her back and the other on her arm as he started walking with Mary out of the bar. Luckily one of Mary's male friends approached the man and assured him that he would take Mary home. The man guffawed but relented. Once Mary got home, she could barely speak and passed out. After a couple days of piecing the night together, Mary felt strongly that the stranger likely slipped something into her drink when he leaned into her. Any drug was likely eliminated from her body and she did not know the stranger's identity, so she never mentioned her suspicions.

THE AMNESIAC EFFECT OF DATE RAPE DRUGS

In the movie *The Hangover,* a group of guys partying in Las Vegas for a bachelor party wake up the next morning with no recollection of the previous night's events. The situation is further complicated by the fact that the groom is nowhere to be found and the men decide the best way to find him is to piece together their evening. One of the men exclaims that this is the worst hangover he has ever had.

Adding up the events of the night includes crashing Mike Tyson's pool, a stint at the hospital for a concussion and an endless amount of partying in Vegas bars. They also learn that one of the friends put what he thought was ecstasy in their drinks, which ended up being Rohypnol. This is the cause for their lack of memory, referred to specifically as **anterograde amnesia** and **retrograde amnesia**. Anterograde amnesia is the loss of memory after the event that triggered the amnesia occurred. In this movie, the men suffered anterograde amnesia after ingesting the Rohypnol. Retrograde amnesia is the loss of memory prior to the event triggering the amnesia. The men had a difficult time putting together the evening because even memories prior to taking the drug were lost. Anterograde and retrograde amnesia are significant biological effects of taking date rape drugs.

NEUROTRANSMITTERS

Every day and every minute, cells in the brain transmit signals that tell our body how to breathe, smile, focus, laugh, run, and stand. The cells responsible for this signaling are called **neurons**. Chemicals in the brain that carry messages between neurons are called **neurotransmitters**. Many medications that treat chronic conditions such as depression, narcolepsy, and attention deficit hyperactivity disorder (ADHD) alter the amounts of neurotransmitters in the brain. One cause of depression is believed to be a lack of serotonin, which is a "feel-good" neurotransmitter. Many antidepressant medications incease the levels of serotonin in the brain, thereby alleviatng depression.

GHB and Rohypnol affect the neurotransmitter **gamma-amino butyric acid**, also known as GABA. GABA is known as a central nervous system depressant. The central nervous system consists of the brain, nerves, and spinal cord. Drugs that enhance the actions of GABA are used to treat seizures and anxiety and are used as sedatives or muscle relaxants.

GAMMA-AMINO BUTYRIC ACID (GABA)

GABA is the neurotransmitter most affected by one of the most commonly used classes of date rape drugs, benzodiazepines. GABA is the most abundant inhibitory neurotransmitter in the brain. Specifically, it helps induce relaxation and sleep. It inhibits overexcitation. GABA contributes to motor control and vision. GABA also regulates anxiety. Some drugs that increase the level of GABA in the brain are used to treat epilepsy and to calm the trembling of people suffering from Huntington's disease.

GHB AND THE PRECURSORS: INCREASING GABA

Of all the date rape drugs discussed in this book, GHB has the most diverse range of physiological effects. Depending on a person's tolerance level, GHB can induce sleep, amnesia, and unconsciousness, increase dopamine and glucose levels, and stimulate growth hormones.

Dopamine is a neurotransmitter that is associated with alertness, focus, and motivation. Dopamine stimulates reward and motivation during pleasurable experiences such as eating and learning. Eating chocolate will trigger cells in the brain to release dopamine. When a pleasurable activity occurs, dopamine molecules then float across the space between the neurons, known as the synapse, where the cells absorb the dopamine, activating signals that translate to "this experience is worth paying attention to." Too much signal and the experience feels unpleasant and overstimulating. Too little, and the experience elicits a yawn; no pleasure, only boredom and distraction.[1]

This process operates like a circuit where the release of chemicals from one set of cells relies on the body's ability to soak up these chemicals with **receptors** to cause the feeling of pleasure or motivation. A properly functioning brain will release and reabsorb (or "reuptake") the proper amounts of dopamine to reward pleasurable activities without overstimulating the body. This system is referred to as the brain's dopamine system. Some people naturally produce weak dopamine signals. It is believed that people who have a dopamine system that produces insufficient dopamine are more likely to become addicted to drugs. Individuals who suffer from lower levels of dopamine might find that they lose interest in activities more quickly, such as with ADHD sufferers. It is not necessary to turn to illegal drugs, because doctors have at their disposal many drugs such as Ritalin that can balance out these brain signaling imbalances.

While it is not clear exactly why GHB can alleviate withdrawal symptoms for heroin addicts and alcoholics, the reason is believed to be due to GHB's effect on dopamine. It is likely that addicts endure decreasing dopamine levels as they withdraw. GHB helps boost these levels, bringing them into the normal range and therefore reducing cravings.

GHB is also believed to increase levels of the neurotransmitters acetylcholine and serotonin. Acetylcholine is a chemical in the brain that enhances sensory perception and helps to sustain attention. Serotonin is a chemical that creates a feeling of satisfaction in the body. The increase of these two neurotransmitters, along with dopamine, are believed to be the cause for the euphoric effect of GHB.

GHB AND NARCOLEPSY

Narcolepsy is a disorder characterized by excessive daytime sleepiness. Narcoleptics can get relief from their symptoms through a special formulation of GHB: Xyrem and taking a stimulant drug during the day. The exact reason that Xyrem taken at night improves wakefulness during the day is not fully understood; however, it likely has to do with the interplay of hormones.

The cause of narcolepsy is likely a combination of genetics and a triggering factor such as an infection that damages the brain. **Hypocretin** is a neurotransmitter that maintains alertness during the day and proper sleep patterns at night. Narcoleptics have low levels of hypocretin. It is likely that a virus or irregular immune response attacks and damages the brain cells that control the production of hypocretin.

Narcolepsy is a rare disorder that often goes undiagnosed for many years. Complaints to a doctor of excessive daytime sleepiness would usually lead to recommendations for getting more sleep rather than testing for narcolepsy, which involves a test of hypocretin levels or overnight brainwave monitoring in a clinic.

The treatment of narcolepsy is most successful when integrated with both medication and behavioral modifications. A couple of different medications are used to keep narcoleptics alert during the day, prevent sudden sleep attacks, and improve sleep at night. Stimulant drugs, such as Ritalin (methylphenidate) and Dexedrine (dextroamphetamine), are used to stay awake during the day and antidepressants are usually successful in preventing a narcoleptic from suddenly falling into REM sleep. Behavioral modifications include getting a full eight hours of sleep each night and taking a nap during the day. Exercise also helps with alertness during the day as long as it does not occur too close to bedtime. Narcolepsy is a chronic condition (it does not have a cure), and so it requires vigilance to limit its negative effect on a person's life. Correctly prescribed, however, Xyrem can greatly improve a narcoleptic's life.

SIDE EFFECTS OF XYREM

Taking any drug presents some level of health risks even under the care of a doctor. The health benefits of taking prescribed drugs ideally outweigh the health risks. Even so, many people stop taking medications due to unpleasant side effects. The most common side effects of taking Xyrem are headache and nausea. To determine side effects and evaluate safety of a drug, the pharmaceutical company will perform a **clinical trial**. A drug company must complete a clinical trial to get FDA approval for its drug. Specifically, a clinical trial is a research study using humans, not animals, to answer health questions, and is conducted in four phases.

Phase I of a clinical trial involves testing the drug on a small group of people for the first time to evaluate its safety, determine appropriate dosage, and identify any side effects. Phase II is a similar process but uses a larger test group of 20 to 300 people. Phase III involves administering the drug to a large group of 300 to 3,000 people to evaluate effectiveness, compare it to commonly used treatments, examine side effects, and basically collect more data to ensure that the drug is safe and effective. Generally, completion of two successful Phase III trials is required for FDA drug approval. In Phase IV clinical trials, studies are completed after the drug has been marketed with the goal of evaluating the drug's effect on different populations and any potential long-term side effects. If harmful effects are discovered in this trial, then the drug may become restricted to certain uses or no longer sold. For instance, Vioxx was an FDA-approved pain-relief drug commonly used to treat arthritis until harmful side effects, specifically risks of heart attack and stroke, were found during this final phase.

Jazz Pharmaceuticals completed clinical trials prior to FDA approval of Xyrem. During these clinical trials, 717 narcoleptic patients took Xyrem. In addition, an additional 443 people participated in the study but received a fake pill or **placebo**, instead of the active drug. Participants who receive the placebo in any experiment are *not* told that the pill they are receiving will have no biological effect. Even though the placebo group receives essentially an inert substance, there will be a response to the mere perception that they are receiving a drug. This response is referred to as the **placebo effect** and is considerable proof of the power of the mind over the body. The group receiving an inert substance will generally have a percentage of people whose condition will improve simply because they believe they are taking a drug—even though they are not. The placebo group is an important tool for researchers to determine exactly how much a drug is having an effect.

During the clinical trials for Xyrem, 10 percent of participants discontinued the trial because of side effects that included nausea, dizziness, and vomiting. Interestingly, 1 percent of those that discontinued were receiving the placebo. Two deaths occurred during the trials from drug overdoses that involved multiple drugs. In one patient, the person taking Xyrem was partly the cause and in another, the person overdosed on multiple drugs not including Xyrem. Other side effects reported by the 717 patients were headache, loss of bladder control, and nasal stuffiness.

ROHYPNOL: A BENZODIAZEPINE

As a benzodiazepine, Rohypnol's main function is as a depressant to the central nervous system. By depressing this area of the body, Rohypnol is likely to induce sleep, amnesia, reduce anxiety, relax muscles, and possibly prevent convulsions in those with a potential for seizures.

In a small percentage of people, benzodiazepines, including Rohypnol, can have the opposite expected effect. Specifically, instead of a tranquilizing effect, the drug may cause the person to become aggressive and even violent. When a drug has the opposite effect, it is referred to as a **paradoxical reaction**. Paradoxical reaction is a phenomenon in **pharmacology** that is possible with almost any drug. It means that the effect rendered in the general population is opposite what occurs in a small percentage of people. It is slightly more likely to occur in children and the elderly. In the case of benzo-diazepines, approximately 5 percent of people will have a paradoxical reaction. The potential for this reaction is slightly higher for short-acting benzos, such as Rohypnol.

The way that Rohypnol exerts its biological change on the body, known as a drug's mechanism of action, is by influencing signaling in the brain. Rohypnol interacts with the signaling of the brain, on neurons called receptors, which cause an increase in the neurotransmitter GABA. Receptors are specialized sites on neurons that accept the neurotransmitter and can be influenced by drugs.

A typical dose of Rohypnol takes effect usually within 15 minutes and lasts up to six hours, longer than GHB. There is only a slim chance that Rohypnol would be detected in the body after 12 hours. It is because of these two reasons that Rohypnol-assisted crimes are hard to prove and easy to commit. The victim is rendered helpless within 15 minutes, develops amnesia, and if at some point the victim suspects he has been drugged, Rohypnol is no longer detectable in urine within three days of taking the drug.

KETAMINE: AN ANTAGONIST

Whereas GHB is considered a depressant, similar to alcohol, ketamine is classified as an antagonist, specifically an NMDA receptor antagonist. An antagonist in pharmacology is a drug that inhibits the action of brain signaling. In the case of a NMDA receptor antagonist, the NMDA receptor does not receive the proper signaling. Depending on the dose, ketamine can act as a stimulant or as a depressant.

When taken recreationally to induce hallucinations, users generally take about 10 to 25 percent of the therapeutic dose required to induce anesthesia. At these low doses ketamine acts more like a stimulant than a sedative and does not usually affect the breathing or heart rate. Each person is different, however, and there have been individuals who have stopped breathing and had their heart stop beating after a small dose of ketamine. If breathing stops and the person is later revived, brain damage is a possible outcome. At very high doses, ketamine behaves more like other anesthetics and can speed up the heart rate and elevate blood pressure.

KETAMINE AND HALLUCINATIONS: HOW THE DRUG AFFECTS BRAIN FUNCTION

Ketamine is a drug that has psychotropic side effects. **Psychotropic drugs**, also referred to as psychoactive drugs, act on the central nervous system, specifically the brain, and alter function in a way that changes mood, consciousness, and perception, often in an extreme enough fashion to cause hallucinations.

Different drugs cause different intensities of hallucinations. The interaction of the hallucinogenic drug and an individual's body chemistry also cause varying intensities of hallucinations in a person. If two people are given the same dose of ketamine, for example, their hallucinogenic experiences, if they have them, will likely be different.

LSD, peyote, psilocybin, and PCP are four other drugs that cause hallucinations. LSD, (an abbreviation for the chemical name, d-lysergic acid diethylamide), was discovered in 1938 and is found naturally in a fungus that grows on rye and other grains. Although it is found naturally, LSD is also manufactured illegally as one of the most potent hallucinogens. Peyote is a small cactus containing mescaline, which causes hallucinations. Psilocybin is found in mushrooms that grow naturally in subtropical regions. Users seeking to get psilocybin's high can grow these mushrooms illegally in a basement. PCP (the abbreviation for the chemical name, phencyclidine), can provoke disturbing hallucinations. It was originally used as an anesthetic but was replaced by ketamine.

Scientists do not know exactly what causes hallucinations but it is believed that the compounds contained in these drugs have chemical structures similar to neurotransmitters. It is believed that the drug compounds disrupt normal brain functioning because of these similarities. Taking hallucinogens is extremely dangerous. Long after the initial hallucinations have subsided—even years later—the user may experience a **"flashback"** (have a hallucination without taking any more drugs)

Despite these risks, many users still experiment and enjoy the escape of psychoactive drugs, including ketamine. Ketamine alters perception in such a way that users liken it to hovering over their body. This "out-of-body" experience is the reason ketamine is defined as a dissociative. By definition, a dissociative drug separates the conscious mind from feelings experienced by the body. An individual who has received enough ketamine to experience this dissociation might view their body being poked, but not experience the pain. This is the reason ketamine can be successfully used during surgery as an anesthetic.

LONG-TERM EFFECTS OF KETAMINE

Continual use of ketamine on a recreational basis can cause alterations to the brain that impair memory, specifically visual memory, verbal memory, and short-term memory. Occasional use of ketamine, just once or twice a month, did not show a reduction in memory, indicating that stopping ketamine might restore full brain function in regards to memory.[2]

A study published in the *British Medical Journal* in 2008 found permanent damage to the bladder as a result of long-term ketamine use.[3] The **bladder** is a hollow organ in the lower abdomen that holds urine. This is consistent with many chronic users' complaints of a need to urinate frequently, pain while urinating, and leakage of urine. As the bladder becomes damaged, scarification occurs, just like a wound on the hand will heal, but if the wound is deep enough, a scar will form. The scar is thicker than regular skin, and the process of damage and scarification of the bladder occurs in a similar fashion. This thickening of the bladder in essence reduces the size and functionality of the bladder, causing symptoms such as frequent urination. It is not clear exactly why ketamine causes bladder damage, and once the bladder has thickened, this is an irreversible condition that the ketamine user must live with forever.

Ketamine users themselves are aware of this link between bladder damage and their drug use. Ketamine users report frequent cramps and pains in the abdomen, so much so that these pains have been labeled "K-pains" or "ketamine cramps." It is also likely that the kidneys are damaged along with the bladder as the kidney attempts to flush the drug out of the body.

The most dangerous risk of long-term ketamine use is the potential for overdose and then death. The longer a ketamine user takes the drug, the more comfortable he may feel with it and less apprehensive about increasing the dose.

DRUG INTERACTIONS AND ALLERGIES

A **drug allergy** is when the body's immune system reacts to a medication as if it is a harmful invader. A drug allergy might cause hives, a rash, or fever, and in rare causes it can be fatal. A drug allergy is one type of adverse medical reaction that specifically involves the immune system.

Benzodiazepines were reported as causing drug allergies as early as 1960. One type of drug allergy reaction that is particularly dangerous is **anaphylaxis**. Anaphylaxis is a severe, whole-body allergic reaction in which airways tighten. Anaphylaxis can be life-threatening. In Canada a case was reported where the use of Ecstasy caused anaphylaxis and was fatal.

When a perpetrator slips a drug into a person's drink, they have no way of knowing if the person could have an unusual reaction to the drug and cause their death.

4
Abuse of Date Rape Drugs

Matt took the advice of one of his bodybuilding friends and started taking a supplement with gamma butyrolactone (GBL), which converts to GHB in the body. Matt took some time to search the Internet for information about the benefits of GBL and felt assured by claims of increased muscle growth, fat burning, and deeper sleep at night.

During the first week Matt took the drug only prior to workouts, and then slowly he began taking it at night to help him sleep. After a week of use he started needing it in the morning to wake up. Usually he diluted the drug and took small sips during class when he felt he needed it, but he found the perfect dose difficult to predict. More than once he experienced the "neck snap" that occurs in users of GHB and its derivatives. During a neck snap, the person's head snaps forward uncontrollably once the GHB takes effect. Matt experienced a neck snap while brushing his teeth. He was knocked unconscious and woke up to find his bathroom mirror cracked and his forehead bleeding.

Matt kept his habit a secret, but his fraternity brothers and family were curious about his odd behavior. He was becoming more withdrawn, irritable, and anxious. He had blackouts and couldn't recall evenings out with friends or driving home in his car.

Matt is considered a GHB addict, also referred to as a "G-aholic." As a bodybuilder, he represents the largest group of people who are GHB addicts. Addiction can happen quickly, sometimes within a few weeks, and detox involves miserable withdrawal symptoms, including profuse sweating, anxiety attacks, and soaring blood pressure and pulse. Once an individual becomes addicted, he will need medical assistance to safely detox from GHB. For those G-aholics who do not try to correct their addiction, their drug use can become fatal.

STAGES OF ABUSE

The abuse of date rape drugs follows a pattern of abuse similar to other drugs. The abuse of drugs begins with experimentation. In the scenario above, Matt likely took GHB for the first time figuring he would just give it a try and see how it felt. In many cases an individual might simply be curious, or perhaps feel they are lacking something in their life and looking for a solution through drugs. In Matt's case he may have felt inferior and wanted GHB to enhance his muscular image.

The next stage in drug abuse is regular use. The drug becomes part of the user's life as he enjoys the effects of the drug, whether it is escape from problems or biological changes to the body, as was the case with Matt. The next stage after regular use is risky use. Not all users of drugs move on to risky use. Many users may stop drug use before they get to this stage, but unfortunately many people, such as Matt, continue to the next stage. Examples of risky use include drinking and driving or having unprotected sex as a result of being on drugs. Research on the use of GHB has shown a greater likelihood of having unprotected sex under the influence of GHB than without. In a 2008 survey in New York, 17 users of GHB were interviewed in depth about their use of GHB. Twelve out of 17 of those surveyed indicated that they had sex while on GHB. Of those that had sex, seven indicated that they had unsafe sex while on GHB, and one person indicated that the only time they had unsafe sex was with GHB.[1]

At the stage of risky use, many people are still able to maintain jobs and personal relationships as they attempt to restrict their drug usage to specific time periods. Addiction, however, is the final stage and one where personal and professional relationships unravel. Addiction is a medical condition that causes psychological and physical dependence; immediate discontinuation of the drug requires medical intervention. **Drug addiction** is an ongoing or chronic disease that involves changes in the brain that result in an irresistible compulsion to use a drug even if the addict understands the consequences to be detrimental. The behavior of addiction is a vicious cycle of increasing cravings and use even with consistent negative consequences. If left untreated, addiction is a condition that continues to negatively affect the well-being of the user. Individuals who have reached the stage of addiction often need medical and psychological intervention to recover. Generally even those individuals who have recovered from addiction will need to resist taking drugs throughout the remainder of their life.

GHB ADDICTION AND WITHDRAWAL

Despite claims on the Internet that GHB is natural and healthy, GHB is highly addictive and potentially fatal. Addiction to GHB can develop in a few weeks. Because GHB is quickly eliminated from the body, addicts must take many doses throughout the day, usually every three hours. Most addicts can not stay asleep without a heavy dose at night.

A typical scenario of someone who has become addicted to GHB usually starts out with occasional use while out with friends. Then the user increases the frequency of her usage to enhance sexual experiences, to wake up in the morning, to sleep at night, to the point that almost every event requires GHB.

Users likely feel that they can stop any time and their usage is not an addiction. They might be in denial about behavioral changes such as explaining frequent periods of blacking out or mysterious bruises and broken bones from neck snaps and drop attacks. Close friends and relatives of the addict may become aware of the problem, and often when they confront the person, the addict becomes distant, thinking he can continue to use the drug without anyone knowing.

GHB addicts are often a danger on the road because GHB affects driving in the same way as alcohol but is not detectable by a Breathalyzer or standard toxicology testing. Law enforcement officers would need to suspect GHB to test for it, and obviously testing would need to be performed within a day of ingestion.

The effects of GHB vary considerably and although GHB is quickly eliminated from the body, it is relatively easy to overdose on GHB. Many addicts either give themselves precise doses throughout the day at specific times so that they do not experience withdrawal or they sip on diluted GHB all day long. In one example provided by the nonprofit Project GHB, a CEO with

Table 4.1 U.S. Emergency Department Mentions for GHB and GBL, 1994–2001	
Year	Total
1994	56
1995	145
1996	638
1997	762
1998	1,282
1999	3,178
2000	4,969
2001	3,340
Source: Substance Abuse and Mental Health Services Administration, Drug Abuse Warning Network	

a GHB addiction gave himself specific doses at particular times during the day. If he had a long meeting to get to at 10 A.M. and needed to give himself a dose at 10:30, he would often take the dose early to make it through the meeting without feeling withdrawal symptoms. The result would be a higher GHB level than he desired, causing a neck snap during the meeting that perplexed his staff.

KETAMINE ADDICTION

Ketamine is a social drug. Those who become addicted might not recognize it is a problem because so many of their friends are doing it at raves and parties. Often, ketamine is a drug for those who seek an extreme way to escape life's problems through the euphoric and out-of-body experience that ketamine provides. Once the continual need to escape eclipses users' ability to maintain proper relationships and a healthy lifestyle, they are addicted.

Ketamine addiction shows signs of wear on the body such as frequent urinary infections, a burning sensation when urinating, as well as an urgency to urinate. The reason for these symptoms is damage to the bladder and kidneys.

Damage to the body is likely to escalate as users continue to take ketamine, partly because the user generally develops tolerance and needs to increase the dosage. In some cases, ketamine users can develop such a high tolerance that they are never able to experience the psychedelic effects of ketamine.

Ketamine does not appear to have the same extent of physical dependence as many other drugs do; however, the psychological dependence from ketamine use is significant. An addict will find the realities of life more difficult to deal with and will continue to seek an altered state through k-trips.

Ketamine addicts will often suffer from flashbacks. Flashbacks are episodes lasting a few seconds where the user re-experiences part of a previous hallucination. The exact biological mechanism of a flashback is not well known. Various hallucinogens cause flashbacks, and the reason may vary for each drug. For some users who take too much ketamine, the hallucination can actually become extremely disturbing (referred to as the "K-hole"). In these cases the flashback might be the result of **posttraumatic stress disorder** (PTSD). PTSD develops after a traumatizing event and is a considered a severe anxiety disorder that includes flashbacks.

In addition to flashbacks, ketamine addicts often suffer from difficulty sleeping, **sleep paralysis**, and **night terrors**. Sleep paralysis occurs when

Table 4.2 U.S. Emergency Department Mentions for Ketamine, 1994–2001	
Year	Total
1994	19
1995	N/A
1996	81
1997	N/A
1998	209
1999	396
2000	263
2001	679
Source: Substance Abuse and Mental Health Services Administration, Drug Abuse Warning Network	

HAVING FUN SAFELY IN COLLEGE

According to the National Institute on Alcohol Abuse and Alcoholism, 88 percent of college students report drinking alcohol. Even without the facilitation of drugs, alcohol remains most often linked to date rape drugs. Alcohol is a depressant, just as date rape drugs are, that can lower inhibitions, cause amnesia, and unconsciousness.

Combining heavy drinking with partying increases not only the chances of sexual assault but also the chance of chance of getting a sexually transmitted disease (STD) as the use of protection decreases with heavy drinking. This is true even in cases of consensual sex. The best way to prevent unwanted consequences from drinking too much alcohol is to drink in moderation—or, of course, not drink at all.

Drinking moderately generally equates to approximately one drink per hour. One drink refers to 1 1/2 ounces of liquor, 12 ounces of beer or 5 ounces of wine; these all contain approximately the same amount of alcohol. In an hour a person's body will likely be able to metabolize the alcohol. The safest bet against being a victim of drug-facilitated rape is to prevent the availability of your beverage to an untrustworthy person: pour your own drink, bring it to the bathroom with you. To be safe, pour it out if you set it down and walk away. Never let someone you do not know well hold your drink for you while you use the bathroom. It is worth repeating that even without the assistance of what we define as date rape drugs, alcohol is by far the most likely accomplice to date rape. Eating before a night out, drinking in moderation, safety in numbers, and keeping control of your drink are the best ways to prevent date rape.

the person is conscious but unable to move the body. Users of GHB have also complained of severe sleep paralysis, when all they could do was blink their eyes while lying down. A night terror is a sleep disorder characterized by extreme fear where the sufferer attempts to waken and eventually does so while screaming, moaning, or gasping. A night terror differs from a nightmare because it does not occur during rapid eye movement sleep and the person can rarely recall the event.

KETAMINE AND BRAIN INJURIES

In May 2004 a high school student named Erin Rose and her boyfriend took ketamine, which they called Special K, for the first time. After a couple of minutes she began convulsing on the floor. She stopped breathing for 18 minutes and was left with a severe brain injury. She was in the hospital for months and had to learn to talk, walk, and even feed herself all over again. Erin can speak, but her speech is halting and difficult to understand. No longer partying with her boyfriend, Erin now speaks out about drug abuse to other young people and how devastating it can be. She admits that one night of taking Special K ruined her life.

Not all people suffer brain damage from taking ketamine but, as with all drugs, the reactions that occur in a person's body cannot be predicted. Even if Erin took the same dose as her boyfriend, he would not necessarily have an adverse reaction, and in this case, Erin was the unlucky one.

ROHYPNOL ADDICTION

While Rohypnol is well known as a mechanism for drug-facilitated rape, the abuse of Rohypnol is most common among attendees at raves and clubs. In addition, heroin and cocaine addicts may use Rohypnol to enhance the high of heroin and mitigate the effects of cocaine.

Rohypnol abusers tend to be men, usually 30 years of age or younger. A study by the Texas Department of State Health Services examined six years of data (1998–2003) regarding calls to the Texas Poison Center Network (TPCN). The TPCN offers 24-hour, 365-day-a-year emergency telephone access to health care information. The hotline receives a variety of phone calls from private individuals and health care workers, whose concerns include a variety of substances both licit and illicit, and even venomous bites.

From 1998 to 2003 the hotline received 620 human exposure calls involving Rohypnol, which represented a small fraction of the total number of calls during that time period (0.07 percent). Of the 620 Rohypnol-related calls, 46.6 percent were from individuals who took the drug for recreational purposes and 14.2 percent were from people who suspected they had taken the drug unknowingly. The remaining calls came from people who were trying to commit suicide or had consumed the drug for an unknown reason. The researchers found that a significantly higher proportion of these calls came from counties that bordered Mexico, which makes sense since the Rohypnol that is present in the United States is brought in from Mexico. Not surprisingly, calls from those who unknowingly took Rohypnol were adult females and those who took the drug recreationally were teen males. Interestingly, in 2003 the number of calls relating to the use of Rohypnol to drug someone decreased. The researchers concluded that while abuse and malicious use calls comprised a large proportion of Rohypnol exposure calls received by Texas poison centers, the number of these calls does not appear to be increasing and may, in fact, be decreasing.[2] The limitations of this type of study are that it is likely that most people who take Rohypnol never call a poison control hotline, so this study does not necessarily extrapolate to the general population of Rohypnol users, but it does shed more light on trends of abuse and suggests that these trends do not seem to be increasing.

ALCOHOL AND DATE RAPE DRUGS

The consumption of date rape drugs is particularly dangerous when combined with alcohol. The enhanced effect of combining drugs and alcohol resulting in a greater intoxicating effect than the sum of each individual drug is known as a **synergistic effect**. Typically, these drugs are ingested along with alcohol for this very reason.

Drinking alcohol also lowers inhibitions, increasing the likelihood that people could be careless about where and with whom they leave their drink. Being intoxicated in a crowded bar or party, with many distractions and feeling less concerned that something could go wrong, may contribute to the potential of a drug-facilitated crime.

Given statistics, it is highly unlikely that advising college students to abstain from alcohol will be well-heeded, but drinking moderately and practicing other safe partying habits can greatly reduce the chances of date rape. The more intoxicated a person becomes, the more likely he or she approaches a state of being taken advantage of sexually.

POLYDRUGGING: WHEN ONE DRUG IS NOT ENOUGH BUT TWICE AS DANGEROUS

Users of drugs often increase the amount and usage of their chosen drug to continue to increase the intensity of their high. Another way of enhancing the drug experience is called polydrugging. Polydrugging is the use of two or more psychoactive drugs to achieve an optimum effect, such as combining alcohol and date rape drugs. Polydrugging is very dangerous because of the difficulty of predicting how drugs will interact in a person's body. In some cases the use of one drug can enhance the effect of the second drug—a type of interaction known as **potentiation.** Individuals who aim for a greater high by combining drugs are often hoping for a synergistic effect. This synergy enhances the effect of both drugs so that the combination of drugs is greater than the total effect of each individual drug if taken independently. More simply put, a synergistic effect is analogous to 1+1=3, rather than 1+1=2.

A user might mix a couple of drugs and not overdose, which could lead to increasingly risky experimentation of combining drugs. On a Web site intended to share personal stories of addiction and recovery, one individual shares the loss of a friend who died as a result of polydrugging. Her friend had dabbled in drugs since her early teens as a temporary escape and to find some happiness. She then moved from marijuana to her drugs of choice: GHB and crystal methamphetamine.

THE DANGERS OF COMBINING DRUGS

Any medication has the potential for side effects. One individual taking a medication could feel dizzy whereas another person might feel drowsy, while yet another person may not experience any side effects.

Combining drugs without knowing the drug interactions can be highly toxic, as it was for Libby. In 1984 Libby was an 18-year-old college student from New York who was taking a prescribed antidepressant, phenelzine, which increases serotonin levels. One evening Libby was partying with friends

Typical of addicts, she moved on to combining even more drugs by adding heroin and a variety of benzodiazepines. Eventually this combination led to an overdose and she died at age 24.

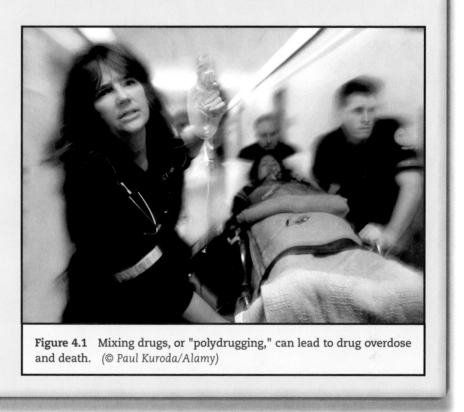

Figure 4.1 Mixing drugs, or "polydrugging," can lead to drug overdose and death. (© Paul Kuroda/Alamy)

and took cocaine, which also increases serotonin levels. Libby developed a fever of 103.5 and went to the hospital. She was given a narcotic painkiller, Demerol, to control her extreme shaking. Demerol, similar to phenelzine, increases serotonin levels. Libby did not tell the emergency room doctors that she had taken any other drug; otherwise, they would not have administered Demerol.

Libby developed serotonin toxicity from these dangerously high levels of serotonin that caused her to become agitated. Forty-five minutes after

Libby was given Demerol, the toxicity caused her to thrash about. The doctor and nurse used a restraining jacket and also tied down Libby's arms and legs to restrain her. Libby was given a sedative but her temperature soared to 108 degrees and she was dead within the next hour. Serotonin toxicity can cause a fever. It was debated in court what exactly killed Libby—the combination of drugs causing a toxic amount of serotonin in her body or an uncontrollable virus. While the exact cause of her death remains unclear, Libby definitely suffered from serotonin toxicity due to taking multiple drugs that increase serotonin levels.

Ketamine, GHB, and Rohypnol (particularly ketamine) are often used as recreational drugs to enter a state of euphoria and escape reality. Someone may begin using drugs only occasionaly, but drug use can quickly become a destructive force in a person's life. When a person continues chronic usage of a drug knowing that such use has negative consequences, he or she has generally entered the phase of addiction. The drugs mentioned in this book cause physical dependence as well as a powerful psychological dependence. Many addicts believe they can stop on their own, but most people need assistance to withdraw safely and stay sober.

5

Date Rape Drugs: Addiction and Treatment

Jake frequently snorted Special K (ketamine) when he went to raves with his friends. He felt safe taking ketamine, figuring it was used by doctors in hospitals to knock people out before surgery. He never took enough to make himself pass out and instead felt a lofty, detached joy that allowed him to enjoy the music, dance freely, and not be annoyed by being jostled by other ravers. Then one night he shared $80 worth of ketamine with a friend, and by the end of the night all he could do was lie on the floor and shake. He recalled everything smelling weird and it reminded him of tripping on LSD.

Usually when on Special K, he only saw mild hallucinations when he was in a dark room with his eyes closed. This time he could not seem to escape the hallucinations that resembled voices, the feeling of falling, and flying, even with the lights swirling around him and his eyes wide open. Jake panicked and wondered if he had taken too much ketamine and caused brain damage. His friends laughed and told him that he had entered the "k-hole," where hallucinations become severe and disturbing, according to users. Users who enter the "k-hole" feel so deep inside their minds and thoughts that they can not escape them, hence the term hole.

A lethal level of ketamine is extremely high, yet smaller doses of ketamine may cause brain damage as well as damage to the kidneys and bladder. Ketamine is addictive. In Jake's situation, treatment for his addiction will be extremely difficult unless he gets professional

65

*assistance. Perhaps even harder, the chance of Jake kicking his habit is
less likely unless he stops socializing with other ketamine users.*

An individual who is addicted to drugs may find it very difficult to regain control over his or her life. Drugs keep people addicted both physically and psychologically. When people use drugs on a regular basis, their body becomes
accustomed to the biological changes that the drug induces. Withdrawal from
a drug addiction is often uncomfortable at best and many times requires medical intervention to safely stop taking a drug.

Another barrier to recovery is the psychological attachment that addicts
have to their drug of choice. For many addicts, drugs such as ketamine are a
coping mechanism for difficulties in life.

DETOXIFICATION AND TREATMENT FACILITIES

In the reality-based TV show *Intervention,* addicts are confronted by their
family and friends, along with the help of the show's interventionist, in hopes
of persuading the person to enter a 90-day treatment program.

In one episode, a woman in her early twenties named Britney is
addicted to heroin with such an expensive habit that she had to perform
sexual acts for drug dealers just to satisfy her addiction. Jobless and living
at home with her mother, Britney has managed to alienate virtually everyone, with only family members still maintaining any hope for her. Her family has asked Britney to get help, but she becomes enraged and resists any
efforts to help. An intervention, which generally occurs as a last resort, is
when the addict's friends and family gather to explain how the other person's addiction has negatively affected their own life and to ask the addict
to please get help. Knowing that many addicts usually have to hit rock bot-
tom before they will agree to stop taking drugs and go to a rehab facility,
participants in an intervention set boundaries of how they will no longer
tolerate the addict's behavior. In some cases, a mother will no longer allow
the addict to live with her. A father might say he will no longer bail out his
child. Friends might say they will no longer take the person's phone calls.
Although harsh, these steps are taken with the knowledge that a person
with a serious drug or alcohol addiction will likely die unless she seeks
treatment.

Figure 5.1 Group therapy is one aspect of substance abuse treatment. *(© David Grossman/Photo Researchers, Inc.)*

Although Britney cried and resisted entering treatment, she eventually relented. Because of Britney's physical dependence on heroin, she was sent to a detox center before being transferred to a treatment facility. A detox center is staffed with nurses and doctors who monitor the patient's medical condition as they withdraw from the drug safely. Patients are usually given medication to ease the withdrawal.

After an addict makes it through detox, the recovery process shifts to their psychological dependence on the drug. The psychological component of addiction can be quite compelling as many addicts have used drugs to cope with painful events in their life. Addicts learn to deal with life's difficulties. Whereas a detox may last a week, full recovery can take months or years. Even after successfully completing detox and treatment, many people still need to transition to a sober living facility before attempting a sober life on their own. A sober living facility provides a drug-free environment usually with residents of the same sex and with the same type of addiction or recovery, for example, drug addiction versus a gambling addiction or an eating disorder. At

New Beginnings Sober Living Facility in Delray Beach, Florida, weekly meetings and guest speakers help to keep residents from relapsing. The biggest challenge for former addicts, however, is when they are thrust back into their former life where temptations exist and life's problems have to be dealt with in new ways. As addiction is a chronic disease, those who have struggled with drugs in the past will generally have a stronger desire to abuse than those who have never become addicted. The challenge is so tough that anywhere from 40 to 60 percent of addicts relapse.

In the case of Britney on A&E's *Intervention,* she abandoned rehab after just one week at the treatment facility and began using again. She was later arrested, went to jail, and then maintained sobriety after her stint in jail.

The treatment of drug addiction is an ongoing process that requires monitoring, just like other chronic diseases such as diabetes and high blood pressure. Someone like Britney will likely need to attend support groups and have a mentor to check in with when she feels the need to use.

Treatment is also a very expensive process. According to the National Substance Abuse Treatment Services Survey (N-SATSS), the average cost for inpatient programs is about $7,000 per month. Many programs are 60 or 90 days long, because programs longer than 30 days generally have higher success rates.

Although the costs of treatment seem high, the cost of substance abuse is far higher. According to the National Institute on Drug Abuse, substance abuse in the United States carries a price tag of half a trillion dollars annually due to health and social costs, such as crime. Drug abuse and criminal activity are linked, and the annual cost to incarcerate a person is approximately $24,000. Every $1 invested in addiction treatment programs yields a return of between $4 and $7 in reduced drug-related crime (including theft) and criminal justice costs. When savings related to health care are included, total savings can exceed costs by a ratio of 12 to 1. Major savings to the individual and to society also stem from fewer interpersonal conflicts, greater workplace productivity, and fewer drug-related accidents, including overdoses and deaths.[1]

LONG-TERM RECOVERY AND RELAPSE

Once an individual becomes addicted to a drug, even if he or she stops the habit for years or decades, there will always be a temptation. One reason for

Figure 5.2 Drug treatment facilities offer an in-patient, intensive treatment setting for those with substance abuse problems. (© Chris Livingston/ Getty Images)

this is that long-term drug abuse results in changes in the brain that persist long after a person stops using drugs. These changes in brain function include an inability to exert control over the impulse to use drugs despite knowing the adverse consequences. The user's life and lifestyle is forever changed by being an addict, and resisting drugs is often a life-long struggle. Drugs present physical and psychological dependence that is difficult to overcome. Often the user must develop new habits and friends that encourage a sober life. Statistics on the relapse rate vary anywhere from 40 to 60 percent.

GHB WITHDRAWAL AND TREATMENT

GHB addicts usually take many doses throughout the day. GHB withdrawal can come on quickly, as quickly as missing a dose by a few hours. Symptoms consist of profuse sweating, delirium, agitation, anxiety attacks, and an increase in blood pressure and heart rate. As a depressant, GHB has a tendency to slow heart rate and blood pressure. The body becomes adjusted to GHB and then when regular dosing is discontinued, the body responds by increasing the heart rate and blood pressure to dangerous levels. During detox, most addicts will be given medication to keep their blood pressure stable.

GHB is similar to many drugs of abuse in that addicts often need medical assistance to safely withdraw. The symptoms of withdrawal can be lessened by administering other drugs such as antipsychotic medications, benzodiazepines (other than GHB, obviously), or phenobarbital. These drugs help to control psychotic agitation. It is crucial that detox occur under the care of a medical professional. Some addicts have attempted to detox on their own and ended up dying. Usually GHB detox, where withdrawal symptoms are strongest, lasts 10 to 14 days.

After a GHB addict safely withdraws, it is a long recovery. Addiction changes the user's body so that removal of GHB leaves them with much higher rates of depression, suicide, anxiety, and difficulty sleeping. Because most addicts had to take GHB to fall asleep, they will likely need to be given an FDA-approved drug to enable them to fall asleep. The incidence of relapse is very high with GHB addicts and often it takes multiple relapses before a GHB addict becomes sober permanently, although temptation will forever be present. Long-term success usually requires support like that provided by groups such as Narcotics Anonymous (NA). Narcotics Anonymous is an international organization that promotes a 12-step program of recovery. NA's recovery program maintains a strong spiritual component and advocates surrender, honesty, and acceptance. Members are encouraged to attend meetings even after they have maintained sobriety. Because NA has chapters available internationally, members have the opportunity to maintain support through attending meetings no matter where they live or where they travel.

Just as addiction involves several phases, so too does recovery. In the beginning, an addict must endure the extreme physical discomfort of withdrawal and will likely need medical intervention to do it safely. Best results for serious addicts is a treatment program that involves counseling and possibly medication to help with cravings. After success at a treatment facility, most former addicts will have the best chance of success by residing in a sober living facility that reduces the chances of temptation. Once addicted, however, the individual will always have some level of craving and will likely need to seek support through a support group such as NA.

Date Rape Drugs and the Law

Travis is a typical college student who enjoys hanging out with his friends and playing hockey. Unfortunately, Travis suffers from narcolepsy, which affects all areas of his life. Narcolepsy is a neurological disorder (a disease that originates in the brain) in which there is a malfunction of sleep cycles. A narcoleptic can fall asleep in the middle of a conversation, class, or even while dancing. Travis has experienced all of these embarrassing situations.

One of the most destructive aspects of his narcolepsy is a condition known as cataplexy. Cataplexy is the sudden weakness of muscle control triggered by laughter, anger, embarrassment, surprise, or any other sudden emotion or event. The backfire of a car can jolt a narcoleptic into cataplexy. At times, cataplexy causes only certain muscles to lose control, such as the neck, resulting in head drooping. Other times, loss of control of many muscle groups makes Travis collapse, even sometimes while playing hockey with his friends. Although Travis appears asleep or unconscious during this state, he can hear and see what is going on around him. The first time it happened, his coach put smelling salts under his nose to try to revive him, causing him pain and driving him further into his cataplexy.

Travis has tried antidepressants to control cataplexy but he didn't like the side effects that caused him to feel lethargic. Travis found success with Xyrem, which is the trade name for the drug sodium oxybate. Xyrem is a form of GHB and was approved by the FDA in 2002 for the treatment of excessive daytime sleepiness and cataplexy in narcoleptics. Travis takes the Xyrem as a liquid at the beginning and middle of the night. The drug helps prevent cataplexy the next day even though it is out of his system by then. Xyrem is strictly controlled for fear of diversion as a date rape drug.

DRUG-INDUCED RAPE PREVENTION AND PUNISHMENT ACT OF 1996

Any person who possesses ketamine, Rohypnol, or GHB with the intent to use it recreationally is already in violation of the law. The Drug-Induced Rape and Prevention and Punishment Act of 1996 mandates up to 20 years in prison for any person who uses a drug on another person to facilitate a crime.

The law specifically mentions Rohypnol, although much of the literature suggests that date rape is more often facilitated with GHB than Rohypnol. Simple possession of Rohypnol holds a possibility of three years' imprisonment, or a fine, or both. The law also includes an educational component whereby police departments receive information on the use of drugs to facilitate rape. It is not clear how effective this law has been in convicting rapists with stiffer penalties for those who use a drug since there are so few successful convictions of date rapists, even those who use Rohypnol, GHB, or ketamine, because it usually becomes an issue of the defendant's word against the victim's. Rohypnol leaves a person so disoriented the next day that by the time he or she has pieced together the previous evening, all traces of the drug have likely vanished from their body. Until better detection procedures are implemented for date rape drugs, many rapists will continue to escape conviction even with laws that carry stiff sentences.

THE HILLORY J. FARIAS AND SAMANTHA REID DATE-RAPE DRUG PROHIBITION ACT OF 2000

In 1999, 15-year-old Samantha Reid and her friends went to a man's apartment in Detroit, along with three young men. The girls were offered drinks. Two of the girls, including Samantha, asked for Mountain Dew and the other girl asked for an alcoholic beverage. The men added either GHB or GBL to their drinks. One of the girls stated that her face felt numb and two of the girls passed out. The third girl complained of difficulty breathing, and the men drove the three girls to the hospital.

On the way to the hospital Samantha stopped breathing. She was put on life support but died 18 hours later. The men were found guilty of poisoning and involuntary manslaughter. They were sentenced to five to 15 years in prison.

Samantha's death resulted in the Hillory J. Farias and Samantha Reid Date-Rape Drug Prohibition Act of 2000, signed by President Clinton. The act caused GHB to be classified as a Schedule I drug. It also involved an educational component that directed the U.S. Department of Health and Human Services to implement a national campaign to educate people about the dangers of GHB. In the past decade, this campaign included launching a new Web site for teens, www.teens.drugabuse.gov, that includes information on GHB and shares stories from teens who have struggled with addiction. In addition, $4 million in grant funds were made available to states and communities to expand drug prevention activities, including GHB abuse.

PUNISHING RAPISTS

The United States is not the only country to prosecute rapists who use GHB, Rohypnol, or ketamine. In British Columbia, Canada, a well-liked pub owner and community hockey manager was arrested in 2007 for spiking women's drinks with GHB and then sexually assaulting them. Those who knew the alleged rapist, 44-year-old Fernando Manuel Alves, were surprised he was capable of spiking the drinks of four women between 20 and 30 years old.

Alves was described as a "regular guy" and generous with his staff at his bar. It is not unusual, however, for rapists who use drugs to appear kind, safe, and respectable. These men are aware that they need to develop some level of trust to initiate contact with their victim.

Canada's case against Alves shows how often these rapists slip through the system. Although Alves was arrested, he quickly made bail and hired a lawyer who criticized the police investigation of his client, insisting that Alves could never be the type of guy to spike a drink. In 2009 Alves ultimately pleaded guilty to only one count of sexual assault after the other assault charges and the administering of GHB were dismissed following a preliminary hearing. Alves ended up getting a nine-month prison sentence.

REGULATION OF GHB, KETAMINE, AND ROHYPNOL

Rohypnol is a drug with a high potential for abuse. Although Rohypnol is a drug that can alleviate insomnia, alternative drugs exist. For this reason, the FDA has opted to make Rohypnol illegal to possess, manufacture, or distribute in the United States, even though it is legal in many other countries.

DRUG SCHEDULING

Even if a drug has a potential for abuse, the FDA may still approve it and will adjust the extent of regulation based on how likely it is to be abused. The way the FDA adjusts restrictions on approved drugs is through **drug schedules**.

The U.S. government ranks drugs in five levels, called schedules, based on their potential for abuse and safety for medical uses. Schedule I drugs have the highest potential for abuse and Schedule V drugs require regulation but have the least potential for abuse. GHB has a high potential for abuse and as a result is listed as a Schedule I drug under the Controlled Substances Act. Heroin is also a Schedule I drug. Ketamine is a Schedule III drug. Morphine, although it is highly addictive, is very beneficial in relieving pain and is therefore a Schedule II drug, even though some people consider it more addictive than heroin.

Requiring a prescription to purchase a drug is one way to control the abuse of a drug. Doctors have the responsibility to monitor and control the dosage and frequency of refills to prevent abuse. In the case of Xyrem, an even more strict distribution program has been instituted because of the potential for abuse.

Even with regulations to control drugs, investigating violations and punishing the violators is a never-ending job for the FDA and the U.S. Drug Enforcement Agency (DEA). Each day, thousands of prescription drugs are illegally imported to the United States. Although regulating these drugs is a crucial part of restricting them, enacting stiff penalties for those who violate drug laws provides the deterrent needed to persuade others not to get involved with distributing date rape drugs.

CONTROLLING GHB

One way that GHB is illegally distributed is by importing a precursor that can then be used to create GHB. This is illegal and the FDA is currently working to locate offenders and prosecute them.

In March 2004 Hadi M. Ghandour, owner of an Internet site that sells drugs, pleaded guilty to four counts of conspiracy to introduce misbranded and unapproved drugs into interstate commerce, counterfeiting human growth hormone, and possessing controlled drugs with intent to distribute during 1999 to 2001. One of the drugs that Ghandour acquired with the intent to sell on his online store was 1,4-butanediol, which converts into GHB. The penalty for these counts is up to five years in prison and a fine of $250,000 on each count.

In an international effort between Canada and the United States called Operation Webslinger, 115 people in 84 cities were arrested for distribution of GHB, GBL, and BD over the Internet. The investigation took two years and involved many agencies including the U.S. Postal Service, U.S. Internal Revenue Service, the DEA, the Royal Canadian Mounted Police, and many others.

Controlling the actions of those who seek to make a big profit from selling popular yet illegal drugs, is a formidable task for the FDA and DEA, primarily due to the proliferation of Internet sites selling these drugs.

Having GBL or BD in a dietary supplement also puts at risk those who do not realize the danger of the compounds they are consuming. Often there are many names for one compound, and most people trust the products they buy in stores, particularly stores that present themselves as health stores. For example, BD may be labeled as sucol-B in dietary supplements. In January 2000 a Utah man died from taking a supplement called Zen that was promoted as a sleep and relaxation aid. He was having sleeping problems and was unaware that Zen contained an addictive and harmful drug when he first began taking the product in 1999. He realized he was addicted and attempted to stop taking Zen before his death. His widow received a settlement from the store that sold him Zen for failure to disclose that the product contained an analog that turns into GHB when consumed.[1]

One of the biggest difficulties of controlling the distribution of GHB is that it can be made at home. Another hurdle for the FDA was the prevalence of GHB and the precursors in dietary supplements. Prior to 1994 the FDA did not have authority over dietary supplements. The Dietary Supplement Health and Education Act of 1994 (DSHEA) amended the federal Food, Drug, and Cosmetic Act to establish a regulatory framework for dietary supplements. The FDA has the authority to remove from the market products that pose a "significant or unreasonable" risk to consumers and that are otherwise adulterated, and to require that labeling for dietary supplements be accurate.

The FDA warned of the dangers of GBL and 1,4-BD in supplements and asked the manufacturers to stop making and distributing these products. The FDA sent warning letters to seven companies that were using GBL in their products. Three of the manufacturers agreed to stop making their GBL-containing supplements. The four remaining companies continued, and faced litigation with the FDA. Some of the companies simply replaced the GBL they were using with 1,4-BD, although there is essentially no difference between the two in terms of risk to health.

ORPHAN DRUGS

Although it is unfortunate to have a medical condition that requires taking a prescription medication, those with a common ailment are in some ways much better off than those who have a rare disorder. The reason for this is that research dollars are focused most on medications that have the greatest potential to make money for a pharmaceutical company. The research, manufacture, and distribution of pharmaceuticals is a private sector, for-profit industry, and to develop and bring a drug to the marketplace often takes years, perhaps a decade, and millions, and in some cases, billions of dollars. A drug company has the best chance of turning a profit if the drug is likely to be purchased by a large number of people. Disorders such as high blood pressure, high cholesterol, and migraines are shared by many people and therefore a lot of research is spent on the development of drugs to cure or manage these conditions.

The result is an increase in quality of life. Twenty years ago migraine sufferers were often prescribed barbiturates to heal their pain, which left the migraine sufferer drowsy and unproductive for the rest of the day. In addition, these medications have a high potential for abuse. Today, migraine sufferers have a choice of many drugs

UNDERCOVER ON THE INTERNET: REVOKING ROOFIES

In July 2000 an agent of the FDA's Office of Criminal Investigations (OCI) went undercover to purchase illegal drugs at a Web site. The agent placed orders via e-mail for a variety of prescription and illegal drugs, including Rohypnol. Once the agent placed the order, he received an invoice for his purchase with instructions to send a money order or cashier's check to Vinci American Ltd. in Las Vegas, Nevada. The drugs were received at the agent's address and had been shipped from Germany to the United States. Documents had been forged to deceive customs and the FDA.

that are not in the barbiturate family and have greatly eliminated the side effect of severe drowsiness, enabling them to cure their migraine and get on with their day.

But what about people who have a rare disease, such a narcoleptic who represents a tiny 0.05 percent of the population versus the 25 percent of women and 8 percent of men who suffer from migraines? It would take a drug company much longer to make a profit from a drug developed to treat narcolepsy versus migraines. Luckily the federal government intervened with the passage of the Orphan Drug Act (ODA) in January 1983. **Orphan drugs** are pharmaceuticals that treat a very small population. Xyrem is an orphan drug. ODA provides incentives for sponsors to develop products for rare diseases. Since the passage of this act, more than 200 drugs and biological products for rare diseases have been brought to market. In the decade before the act was passed, fewer than 10 such products came to market.

Without the incentives provided to drug companies through the ODA, people suffering from rare diseases would find little relief in the current drug market to heal their disorder. The ODA is one way the federal government has been able to intervene and improve the quality of life for people when there is little market-driven incentive for drug companies.

The owner of the Web site was Christian Frederic Finze, a businessman in his early forties. Finze set up the drug distribution company in Germany with the intent of importing the drugs illegally to the United States. During the investigation OCI discovered 7,200 units of Rohypnol, antibiotics, anti-allergenics, weight loss medications, steroids, and hormones. The estimated value of the controlled substances was more than $400,000.

Finze pleaded guilty to various counts of conspiracy, distribution, and importation of controlled substances. In 2005 the 46-year-old Finze had yet to be sentenced due to extensive health problems that caused him to enter the courtroom in a wheelchair and appear with a softball-sized lump on his elbow. Later that year, however, Finze was sentenced to 120 months in federal prison.

Internet pharmacies selling illegal drugs or prescription drugs without a prescription that are based in foreign countries are nearly impossible to control, but pharmacies clearly based in the United States are more easily held to FDA and DEA standards, as was Finze.

STOREFRONT PHARMACIES

In Chicago a pharmacy called Rx Depot Inc. proudly boasted of assisting customers with discount drugs by importing them from Canada. Rx Depot Inc. had stores not only in Chicago but all across the United States. It was a profitable chain aimed at consumers looking to save costs on prescriptions. Unlike Internet-based pharmacies that import illegal substances and try to hide it, Rx Depot Inc. was open about its protocols, originally without fear of prosecution.

RxDepot Inc. is just one of many storefront pharmacies that operate as a walk-in business to make it easy for customers to purchase prescription drugs over the Internet. The FDA became concerned that these pharmacies were a threat to public health because unapproved prescription drugs were being imported. Rx Depot Inc. and other similar pharmacies have stated that the FDA approves of their activities and that the drugs are FDA approved, even though many of them are not, such as Rohypnol.

In September 2003 the FDA filed an injunction to stop Rx Depot Inc. from importing drugs from Canada, essentially ordering that the chain be shut down. The FDA was successful and Rx Depot Inc. is no longer able to import drugs that are not FDA-approved.

KETAMINE RAIDS

In March 2010 detectives in New York City raided a network of single-family homes where people were illegally selling prescription drugs, including ketamine. The police department's Narcotics Bureau arrested more than two dozen people for selling Vicodin (hydrocodone), oxycodone, Suboxone (buprenorphine), codeine, Adderall (amphetamine) and ketamine, as well as other seriously addictive drugs, the authorities said. Vicodin, oxycodone, and Suboxone are all drugs in the opiate family with a high potential for abuse. Adderall is a stimulant drug used to treat attention-deficit/hyperactivity disorder (ADHD).

Law enforcement has seen an increase in the abuse of prescription drugs, particularly OxyContin, Vicodin, and Percocet. One of the reasons is that these drugs are prescribed legally, so they can be more easily purchased than drugs that are not approved for any use in the United States, such as heroin.

WHEN DANGEROUS DRUGS CAN HEAL

Properly prescribed, drugs are meant to improve the quality of life, but when drugs are misused they can destroy a person's health. Medicine seeks to find a balance between creating drugs to enhance life and preventing these drugs from being diverted for illicit purposes. Heroin has legitimate uses as a pain-killer, yet the potential for abuse is so high that it is no longer used for this purpose. Instead, heroin has been replaced with other drugs that have a lower potential for abuse.

Illicit drug use is prevented through a variety of regulating systems. The most common system is requiring a prescription. Another way to reduce the potential for abuse is to alter the formulation of the drug so that it is released into the body in staggered doses. In April 2010 the FDA approved a new formulation of OxyContin (oxycodone) aimed to reduce abuse. Oxy-Contin was approved by the FDA in 1995 and is quite successful at alleviating pain. Similar to heroin, OxyContin is in the opiate family of drugs that produces euphoria as a side effect. Since its approval in 1995, OxyContin has always been formulated to reduce the opportunity for abuse based on the controlled-release formulation. A controlled-release formulation staggers the amount of the drug that is released in the body. Controlled-release or extended-release formulations are generally more convenient because the patient needs to take fewer pills throughout the day. As with almost every system in place to prevent abuse, there are ways around it. In the case of OxyContin, users looking to abuse the drug either cut up the pill, chew it, or dissolve it to release high levels of oxycodone all at once to achieve their euphoric high.

The reformulated version of OxyContin produces a gummy substance when it is dissolved so that it cannot be drawn up into a syringe or injected. The new formulation is an attempt to reduce abuse, but eliminating all potential for abuse is impossible.

THE XYREM SUCCESS PROGRAM

The approval of Xyrem (sodium oxybate) by the FDA in July 2002 to treat cataplexy was life-changing for narcoleptics who suffered from cataplexy. With the potential of suddenly losing muscle control, many narcoleptics were restricted from driving a car and holding down many types of jobs. Xyrem clearly improves the quality of life for narcoleptics.

In closely monitored clinical trials of Xyrem, there was a low incidence of abuse. According to the FDA, GHB prescribed for therapeutic uses has a low risk of abuse when compared to other drugs, such as antidepressants.

Unfortunately, the approval of Xyrem creates the possibility that the drug will be misused as either a date rape drug or as a recreational drug. The Xyrem Success Program was created to address these concerns. One feature of this program is a restricted drug distribution system. With other prescription medications, a manufacturing facility distributes the drug to multiple wholesalers. These wholesalers then distribute the drug to retail pharmacies. Currently, there are approximately 63,000 registered retail pharmacies. Individuals go to their doctor to get a prescription and then go to the retail pharmacy to get the drug. Patients can consult with the pharmacist if they have questions, and information about the drug is supplied.

The distribution of Xyrem is much different. The manufacture of Xyrem is confined to just one facility. Instead of a choice of 63,000 retail pharmacies, only one specialty pharmacy distributes the Xyrem to the patient via an overnight courier such as FedEx.

The Xyrem Success Program includes a physician and patient registry. Once the specialty pharmacy receives a prescription for Xyrem on a prescription form unique to Xyrem, the pharmacy assigns the patient to a dedicated pharmacy team. The specialty pharmacy also verifies that the physician is eligible to prescribe Xyrem and follows up with a phone call to verify that the doctor did indeed fax a prescription to the pharmacy. The pharmacy then calls the patient to verify his or her address and make sure the patient understands that Xyrem will be arriving by overnight courier. The team also explains the concern of Xyrem being diverted for illegal uses. There are only nine other FDA-approved drugs that have a risk-management component.

The FDA believes this risk-management program has helped prevent the diversion of Xyrem as a source of GHB and in fact reports that there is no indication that GHB is being diverted as a result of the approval of Xyrem. In addition, the amount of GHB manufactured as a result of approving Xyrem is relatively small compared with other sources of GHB such as precursors of GHB and is therefore not a focus of those seeking an illegal use of GHB.

THE ROOFIES TRAIL: FROM MEXICO TO THE SOUTHERN UNITED STATES

Amber was enjoying spring break in Cancun, Mexico. It had been a grueling freshman year at college and she was soaking up every minute of sun, sand, and relaxation. The evenings generally turned a bit more rowdy as her sorority sisters bought her shots while they all danced in crowded clubs.

At one point, one of her friends passed around little green pills that her friend claimed would enhance the party experience. Amber was a bit unsure since she did not usually take drugs, but everyone was doing it and she did not want to stand out. Always a little shy, Amber never really felt secure about her dancing in public. After taking some of the green pills, she felt so calm and happy that she really enjoyed her evening.

The next morning, Amber's memory was a little foggy but she recalled having a good time and feeling less inhibited than usual. That day, while out with her friends, she was able to get some more of the green pills that she learned were called roofies. She had never heard of them but was told they were legal in most countries to treat insomnia. Amber often suffered from insomnia due to worrying about her grades. In Mexico she was able to get a year's supply of the pills, enough to hold her over until her next spring break. When returning to the United States, Amber chose to hide the pills in the soles of her shoes, but she was told that she would need only a doctor's prescription in Mexico to be able to legally declare the pills at customs.

Amber's situation is just one of the ways that Rohypnol enters the United States. According to a University of Texas study, 43 percent of the people declaring prescription drugs over a one-year period at a Mexican border were importing Rohypnol.[2]

It is illegal to manufacture, possess, or distribute Rohypnol in the United States, but because this drug is manufactured in other countries, it is easily imported. Most of the Rohypnol that enters the United States is purchased in Mexico and is then trafficked into the United States primarily through Miami and the southern United States. In the early 1990s it was legal to import Rohypnol from a country that permits its legal use. With a valid prescription, a person was allowed to bring in a three-month supply. As of this writing Rohypnol may no longer be imported even from a country where it is legal or with a doctor's prescription. In March 1996 the importation of Rohypnol was prohibited by the U.S. government based on its growing abuse by American teens and college students. Rohypnol, however, still finds its way easily through borders.

7

Date Rape Drugs: Future Trends

A 19-year-old French woman believed her soft drink had been spiked and that she was sexually assaulted. She had no memory of the crime but went to the police five days later. Knowing that any trace of most date rape drugs would likely not be detected in blood and urine, the police contacted a lab known for detecting drugs in hair samples.

The scientists at the lab told the police to advise the teenager to grow her hair for one month without cutting it. This length of time would allow sufficient analysis to detect any date rape drugs. After one month, full-length hair samples 8 centimeters long were taken from the girl. Analysis at the lab detected an increase of GHB concentrations at the time corresponding with the teen's allegation of rape.

The girl was able to identify her rapist, who was unaware of the investigation. The police apprehended the man and provided the evidence. The rapist was arrested and did not challenge the findings.[1]

DETECTING DRUGS IN HAIR SAMPLES

One of the greatest challenges to proving a drug-facilitated crime is that the drugs are quickly eliminated from the body. Often by the time someone reports, or even suspects, a crime has been committed, there is no evidence—with the exception of hair.

Scientists have been successful in proving drug exposure by analyzing hair samples. In one documented scenario a 39-year-old woman having marital problems felt sleepy for 24 hours after consuming a cup of coffee at home.

83

A blood sample was collected 20 hours after the woman had the coffee. The blood test detected **bromazepam**, whereas the hair sample was bromazepam free. Bromazepam is a benzodiazepine that causes sedation and is used for the short-term treatment of panic attacks. Another strand of hair was collected from the woman approximately one month after the event, and 2 centimeters of the hair strand tested positive for bromazepam, whereas the area of the hair below and above that 2 centimeters tested negative for bromazepam. Detection of a drug in the middle of the hair strand is consistent with a single exposure of a drug, confirming the wife's suspicions that she had been drugged by her husband. The coffee cup also tested positive for bromazepam.[2] It was not clear from the report why the husband chose to drug his wife, but the evidence implicated him.

With the use of hair analysis, nearly almost any drug can be detected. Scientists have used this procedure in situations where a caretaker is suspected of unlawfully sedating children. In one situation a nurse administered niaprazine, a hypnotic, to six children that were under her care. The nurse's motive was to keep them quiet.

Hair analysis is also successful in detecting the poisoning of a child by the parent to keep the child ill, a mental illness called **Munchausen syndrome by proxy**. In this syndrome, a parent intentionally inflicts medical harm on his or her child, such as by poisoning, in an effort to gain sympathy. Taking a hair sample for analysis can confirm whether a child is suffering under the hands of the parent. In one documented case an 18-month-old, the youngest daughter in a family of five children, suddenly became weak and unable to stand, was choking, and then became unconscious. Her parents rushed her to the hospital where numerous tests were performed. The girl's condition improved, but doctors were not able to give a clear reason for the child's sudden illness. The child went home with the parents after staying in the hospital for several days, but the cycle repeated itself when the child again became ill at home and then was rushed to the hospital. Eventually, during one of the periods of sudden illness when the child became unconscious, she was unable to be revived. An autopsy revealed that the child died of heart failure.

Six weeks later the older sister fell ill with the same signs, and doctors suspected a hereditary heart defect similar to her younger sister's. The older sister was hospitalized for two months while doctors performed tests, yet they were not able to diagnose her illness. The girl was sent home and the cycle

"DRINK DETECTIVE": DATE RAPE DRUG DETECTION

The Drink Detective is a kit consisting of a dropper, three pieces of paper, and a couple of bottles of solution along with directions to test your beverage. First, the dropper is used to take a sample of the drink. The sample is then squirted on a piece of paper labeled as the G paper. If the paper turns blue then the drink contains GHB. The next piece of paper is the K paper. If the K paper turns red or pink, then the drink contains ketamine. Finally, if a sample of the drink creates two lines on the B paper, then the drink contains benzodiazepines.

The Drink Detective is said to have a high rate of success, but false positives can occur. A bigger barrier to the success of the Drink Detective is the labor-intensive process of extracting multiple samples and placing the samples on tiny pieces of paper in the midst of a party or crowded bar, while precisely following a set of written instructions. The odds of accurately following the directions likely decrease if the person continues consuming alcohol.

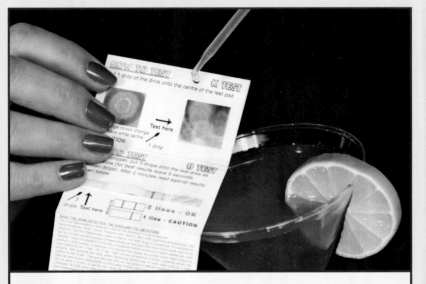

Figure 7.1 Date rape drug detection kit. *(© Graeme Robertson/Getty Images)*

of illness and hospitalization continued. In a 10-month period, the daughter was hospitalized 10 times. In the last visit to the hospital, clozapine was detected in the child's urine. Clozapine is a drug used to treat schizophrenia that has unwanted side effects, including adverse cardiovascular and respiratory effects. Doctors suspected this was a case of Munchausen syndrome by proxy and had the youngest child's body exhumed to test for the presence of clozapine. After 10 months of the child's body in a soil grave, only hair could be tested for clozapine. The deceased child's hair tested positive. Upon being presented with this information, the mother confessed, and she was later sentenced.[3]

Surreptitious poisoning can be done by strangers, friends, and family. Hair analysis for the identification of drug-facilitated crimes is becoming more accepted as a means of diagnosing a mysterious illness or a suspicion of sexual assault when a substantial amount of time has elapsed since the crime.

DETECTING GHB IN SALIVA

Testing for date rape drugs currently involves testing blood, urine, and, to a lesser extent, hair. Testing saliva for date rape drugs offers the advantage of being able to perform testing in public. Urine and blood require a level of privacy as well as trained medical personnel. Testing hair for date rape drugs presents a lengthy wait time. Saliva can be obtained easily and without the expertise of a highly trained individual.

The process whereby saliva can be analyzed to detect GHB is called high-field, high-resolution nuclear magnetic resonance (NMR). NMR is a complex area of science that has made many significant advances in the last 25 years. NMR can be used to identify a wide range of compounds in both a liquid and solid state. In studies performed by London South Bank University, NMR was found to be a very reliable method of identifying GHB in saliva and in beverages.[4]

EXPANDING LEGITIMATE USES OF ILLICIT DRUGS

Xyrem is an example of a formerly illegal drug that was able to be FDA-approved by fine-tuning a distribution system that involves only one manufacturer that ships the drug overnight to the patient. Based on follow-up by the maker of Xyrem, Jazz Pharmaceuticals, the approval and legal distribution of this drug has largely been confined to the intended purpose.

Usually a drug is initially developed to primarily treat one disorder. Eventually, as the drug is used by the public, it is often found helpful in treating other disorders. For example, Topomax (topiramate) is a drug that was FDA approved in 1995 to treat seizures. The drug was subsequently found to help prevent migraines. It is now FDA approved as a daily medication to prevent migraines.

INTERNATIONAL DRUG TRAFFICKING TRENDS

The Internet has greatly increased the availability of illegal drugs. To successfully control date rape drugs, laws must override political boundaries as international organizations strategize to keep everyone safe and punish distributors. Laws and regulations enacted by the United States have little, if any, muscle against an Internet-based pharmacy based in Africa.

As death and disabilities mount from ketamine, Rohypnol, and GHB, as well as GBL and 1,4-DB, the international community has responded with international organizations such as the International Narcotics Control Board (INCB). In May 2010 INCB vowed to address the use of benzodiazepines and substances not under international control to commit sexual assault. Some of the actions presented by INCB include raising awareness among the general public, alerting law enforcement agencies to such practices so that they can take measures to detect the presence of date rape drugs in victims, and inviting the cooperation of industry, for example, to facilitate the detection of such substances in drinks before they are consumed, as was accomplished by adding blue dye to Rohypnol.

BUILDING AWARENESS

Illegal drug trafficking and consumption will likely always exist. One way to help control the abuse of drugs is to educate the people who are a target for drug dealers. For some people, even one night of drug use can alter their lives forever, as was the case with high school student Erin Rose, who was left permanently brain damaged after taking ketamine with her boyfriend. Although many people associate Rohypnol with date rape, the general public is probably not aware of the current death and disability toll from GHB, ketamine, and Rohypnol.

As an example, GHB is one drug where awareness of the drug's potentially disastrous effects is much needed to counter the misinformation that is spread by GHB manufacturers and sellers on the Internet. One successful campaign is Project GHB, which aims to provide accurate information on the Internet through its Web site, www.projectghb.org. Project GHB was initiated by the parents of Caleb Shortridge, who died at the age of 27 after taking GHB in 1998. Caleb had a few friends over to his San Diego apartment. One of the friends was a GHB dealer. When Caleb's roommate, Sarah, came home, she noticed that Caleb was passed out and asked what happened. The drug dealer laughed and told her he drank GHB, thinking it was water. Sarah asked if they should call the hospital and the drug dealer said not to bother, that Caleb would just sleep it off. Sarah continued to check on him throughout the evening, and he did appear to be sleeping—when she poked him, he would snore. At around 10:30 P.M., Sarah checked on him again and he did not seem to be breathing, so she called 911 and began CPR. The paramedics were able to get a faint pulse in the ambulance, but it quickly faded and Caleb died. It was approximately four or five hours after Caleb ingested the GHB that he died. The medical examiner said that his levels were the highest she had ever seen. A typical dose of GHB is a capful; Caleb likely took a far greater amount than that if he drank it as though he believed it was water. Caleb's death was ruled an accident.

Since Caleb's death his parents have worked to educate people about the dangers of GHB through Project GHB. At the time of Caleb's death they felt that there were not any Web sites dedicated to the truth of GHB, and they used the forum to highlight Caleb's death as well as those of many others who died from taking GHB or a derivative. The Web site has branched out to include information about other drugs such as ketamine and Ecstasy. Project GHB is a nonprofit group that has grown to include a staff beyond Caleb's parents. Outreach is an important tool in any antidrug campaign.

SUMMARY

Controlling the manufacture, use, and distribution of ketamine, GHB (and its analogs), and Rohypnol is an ongoing challenge for the agencies that seek to protect human health and prosecute criminal behavior. Advances in chemistry have improved lives, such as Xyrem for narcoleptics and BD for the plastics industry, yet in the wrong hands, these chemicals can be used to facilitate crimes.

Providing reasonable access to these compounds without diversion to harmful uses is the reason for drug scheduling, laws that allow for stiffer penalties, and, in the case of Xyrem, a drug distribution schedule that lessens the chance that anyone other than a narcoleptic will have access to Xyrem.

The Internet will be a continual source of illegal drugs as online sellers devise new deceptive tactics to thwart enforcement efforts. With the assistance of international organizations such as INCB, efforts can be redoubled to stem the flood of illicit drugs.

The difficulty of regulating GHB, ketamine, and Rohypnol is further complicated by the issue of establishing the incidence of drug-facilitated date rape. Statistics vary, and the incidence of women reporting that they believe they were drugged versus sexual assault victims testing positive for date rape drugs are highly disproportionate. Many people claim that the incidence of drug-facilitated date rape is actually very low, and insist that merely the alcohol, not a drug, incapacitated the victim. It is also highly likely that women are being drugged, but the combination of amnesia and embarrassment makes a victim hesitate just long enough that the drug is eliminated from the body. The number of women who actually report date rape, under any circumstances, is likely quite low, compared with actual date rape.

The best way to reduce drug-facilitated date rape is through education, drug regulations, and enforcement. For those who choose to take ketamine, Rohypnol, and GHB recreationally, education is also crucial in preventing users from destroying their life through drug addiction.

Notes

Chapter 1

1. Burkhard Madea and Frank Musshoff, "Knock-Out Drugs: Their Prevalence, Modes of Action, and Means of Detection," *Deutsches Aerzteblatt International* 106, 20 (2009): 341–347.

2. Amanda Hess, "The Date Rape Drug Is an Urban Myth: Let's Put It to Rest," *Washington City Paper*, http://www.washingtoncitypaper.com/blogs/sexist/2009/10/28/the-date-rape-drug-is-in-an-urban-myth-lets-put-it-to-rest/ (posted October 28, 2009).

3. Nursing Standard, "Advice for Nurses on Drug-related Sexual Assault," *Nursing Standard* 21, 12 (2006): 11.

4. U.S. Department of Justice/National Drug Intelligence Center, "GHB Analogs: GBL, BD, GHV, and GVL," *Information Bulletin,* Product No. 2002-L0424-003, August 2002.

5. Christine Saum and James A. Inciardi, "Rohypnol Misuse in the United States." *Substance Use and Misuse* 32, 6 (1997): 724.

6. Richard Schwartz and Regina Milteer, "Drug-Facilitated Sexual Assault," *Southern Medical Journal* 93, 6 (2000): 558–561.

7. Adam Negrusz and R.E. Gaensslen, "Analytical Developments in Toxicological Investigation of Drug-facilitated Sexual Assault," *Analytical and Bioanalytical Chemistry* 376 (2003): 1192–1197.

8. Steven Lee and Petros Levounis, "Gamma Hydroxybutyrate: An Ethnographic Study of Recreational Use and Abuse," *Journal of Psychoactive Drugs* 40, 3 (2008): 245–253.

9. U.S. Department of Justice/National Drug Intelligence Center, "GHB Analogs: GBL, BD, GHV, and GVL," *Information Bulletin,* Product No. 2002-L0424-003, August 2002.

10. Nicholas Reuter, "Scheduling of Drugs Under the Controlled Substances Act," Congressional Testimony 1999, http://www.fda.gov/NewsEvents/

Testimony/ucm115087.htm (posted March 11, 1999).

11. Richard Schwartz and Regina Milteer, "Drug-Facilitated Sexual Assault," *Southern Medical Journal* 93, 6 (2000): 558–561.

12. Steven Lee and Petros Levounis, "Gamma Hydroxybutyrate: An Ethnographic Study of Recreational Use and Abuse," *Journal of Psychoactive Drugs* 40, 3 (2008): 245–253.

13. David E. Fuller and Carl S. Hornfeldt, "Alternative Viewpoints: From Club Drug to Orphan Drug: Sodium Oxybate (Xyrem) for the Treatment of Cataplexy," *Pharmacotherapy* 23, 4 (2003): 1205.

14. John F. Cryan and Olivia F. O'Leary, "A Glutamate Pathway to Faster-Acting Antidepressants," *Science* 329 (2010): 913-914.

15. David E. Fuller and Carl S. Hornfeldt, "From Club Drug to Orphan Drug: Sodium Oxybate (Xyrem) for the Treatment of Cataplexy," *Pharmacotherapy* 23, 9 (2003): 1205–1209.

16. Trinka Porrata, "Ketamine," The GHB Project, http://www.projectghb.org/2008/ketamine.php (accessed May 1, 2010).

Chapter 2

1. Michael Cohn, "GHB and Alcoholism," *The New*

Lycaeum, http://www.lycaeum.org/~ghbfaq/alcoholism.html (Downloaded May 2, 2010).

2. "Using GHB to Mitigate Opiate Withdrawal," *The New Lycaeum*, http://www.lycaeum.org/leda/docs/10243.shtml?id+10243 (posted September 21, 2000).

3. E. Krupitsky et al., "Ketamine Psychotherapy for Heroin Addiction: Immediate Effects and Two-year Follow-up," *Journal of Substance Abuse and Treatment* 23, 4 (2002): 273–283.

Chapter 3

1. Brian Vastag, "Pay Attention: Ritalin Acts Much like Cocaine," *Journal of the American Medical Association* 286, 8 (2001): 905–906.

2. Celia J. Morgan, Leslie Muetzelfeldt, and Valerie Curran, "Consequences of Chronic Ketamine Self-administration upon Neurocognitive Function and Psychological Well-being: A 1-year Longitudinal Study," *Addiction* 105, 121 (2009): 1360.

3. A. Cottrell et al., "Urinary Tract Disease Associated with Chronic Ketamine Use," *British Medical Journal* 336 (2008): 973.

Chapter 4

1. Steven Lee and Petros Levounis, "Gamma Hydroxybutyrate: An Ethnographic Study of Recreational Use and Abuse," *Journal of Psychoactive Drugs* 40, 3 (2008): 245–253.
2. Mathias B. Forrester, "Flunitrazepam Abuse and Malicious Use in Texas, 1998–2003," *Substance Use and Misuse,* 41 (2006): 297–306.

Chapter 5

1. National Institutes of Health/National Institute on Drug Abuse, *Principles of Drug Addiction Treatment: A Research Based Guide,* http://www.drugabuse.gov/podat/faqs.html (accessed May 24, 2010).

Chapter 6

1. U.S. Department of Justice/National Drug Intelligence Center, "GHB Analogs: GBL, BD, GHV, and GVL," *Information Bulletin,* Product No. 2002-L0424-003, August 2002.
2. Christine Saum and James A. Inciardi, "Rohypnol Misuse in the United States," *Substance Use and Misuse* 32, 6 (1997): 723–731.

Chapter 7

1. Pascal Kintz, "Bioanalytical Procedures for Detection of Chemical Agents in Hair in the Case of Drug-facilitated Crimes," *Analytical and Bioanalytical Chemistry* 388 (2007): 1469.
2. Ibid.
3. Christine Bartsch et al., "Munchausen Syndrome By Proxy (MSBP): An Extreme Form of Child Abuse with a Special Forensic Challenge," *Forensic Science International* 137 (2003): 147–151.
4. Martin Grootveld et al., "Determination of the Illicit Drug Gamma-hydroxybutyrate (GHB) in Human Saliva and Beverages by H NMR Analysis," *BioFactors* 27 (2006): 121–136.

Glossary

1,4-butanediol (1,4-BD or BD)   a precursor of GHB that converts to GHB in the body

additive effect   the effect of two drugs taken together where the total effect equals the sum of the individual effects

analgesic   painkiller

analog   compounds that that have structural chemical similarity

anaphylaxis   a severe, sometimes life-threatening, whole-body allergic reaction during which airways tighten, restricting the ability to breathe

anterograde amnesia   the loss of memory after the event that triggered the amnesia occurred

benzodiazepines   a group of drugs known for their sedating effect. Rohypnol and Valium are benzodiazepines.

bladder   the hollow organ in the lower abdomen that holds urine

bromazepam   a benzodiazepine that is used for the short-term treatment of panic attacks

cataplexy   the sudden weakness of muscle control triggered by laughter, anger, embarrassment, surprise, or any other sudden emotion or event

central nervous system (CNS)   the brain, nerves, and spinal cord

central nervous system depressants   drugs that slow down mental or physical functions such as blood pressure and heart rate

central nervous system stimulants   drugs that speed up mental or physical functions

clinical trial   a research study that uses a drug on humans to answer health questions; required before a manufacturer can submit a drug for FDA approval

cognitive functioning   the ability of a person to use reason and judgment, show awareness, and maintain proper perception

control group   participants in an experiment who do not receive the drug being tested

dopamine   a neurotransmitter that stimulates reward and motivation during pleasurable experiences such as eating and learning

double blind experiment   A scientific experiment in which neither the patient nor the person giving the drug knows which pills represent the drug being tested or the placebo.

drop attack   when a person who has consumed GHB suddenly loses muscle control and drops to the floor

drug addiction   a chronic disease involving changes in the brain that result in an irresistible compulsion to use a drug

drug allergy   when the body's immune system reacts to a medication as if it is a harmful invader

drug schedules   the U.S. government ranks drugs in five levels, called schedules, based on potential for abuse and safety for medical uses

euphoria   a feeling of intense well-being

flashback   an episode lasting a few seconds where the user re-experiences part of a previous hallucination

gamma-amino butyric acid (GABA)   a neurotransmitter important in regulating overexcitation; drugs that enhance GABA production are used to treat anxiety and insomnia

gamma butyrolactone (GBL)   a precursor of GHB that converts to GHB in the body

GBL   abbreviated chemical name for gamma butyrolactone, which is a precursor for GHB

GHB   abbreviated chemical name for gamma hydroxybutyrate, which is used as a date rape drug, club drug, and as a treatment for narcolepsy

hallucinations   significant distortions of reality during which a person believes he or she is seeing, feeling, and hearing images, sensations, and sounds that are not real

hypocretin   a neurotransmitter that maintains alertness during the day and proper sleep patterns at night

ketamine   a drug legitimately used as an animal tranquilizer that has been diverted for illicit use as a recreational drug and to facilitate date rape

mechanism of action   the biological mechanism through which a drug produces its beneficial effect

methylprylone   a sedative in the piperidinedione family of drugs that has been replaced in use by better-performing benzodiazepines

mirror neurons   brain cells that react when a person moves and also when one person watches another person move

Munchausen syndrome by proxy   a psychological disorder whereby a parent intentionally inflicts medical harm on his or her child, such as by poisoning, in an effort to gain sympathy

narcolepsy   a neurological disorder in which sleep-wake cycles are disturbed to the extent that the individual cannot stay awake during normal daily activities

neck snaps   a phenomenon experienced by GHB users where their neck suddenly snaps forward after taking too much GHB

neurons   cells in the brain and spinal cord that transmit information

neurotransmitters   chemicals in the brain that act as messengers between neurons

night terror   a sleep disorder characterized by extreme fear; when sufferers awaken they usually do so while screaming, moaning, or gasping

orphan drugs   pharmaceuticals such as Xyrem that treat a very small population

paradoxical reaction   when a drug has the opposite effect than that which is intended

pharmacology   the science of drugs; specifically their therapeutic value

placebo   an inert substance, such as a sugar pill, that is administered to a control group

placebo effect   the tendency of an inert medication (a placebo) to have a beneficial effect on the recipient simply because he or she believes that it will work

polydrugging   the use of two or more psychoactive drugs to achieve a desired effect, such as combining alcohol and date rape drugs

posttraumatic stress disorder (PTSD)   a severe anxiety disorder that develops after a traumatizing event and often includes flashbacks

potentiation   a type of drug interaction in which one drug enhances the effect of another drug

prolactin　a hormone that is associated with the production of milk in the body (lactation)

psychotherapy　sessions with a therapist to treat psychological and emotional disorders

psychotropic drug　a drug that changes mood, consciousness, and perception; some psychotropic drugs may cause hallucinations

receptors　specialized sites on neurons that accept the neurotransmitter and can be influenced by drugs

REM sleep　phase of sleep associated with rapid eye movement (REM) and dreaming

retrograde amnesia　loss of memory prior to the event that triggered the amnesia

Rohypnol　a sedative, illegal in the United States, that is used recreationally and to facilitate date rape

serotonin　a neurotransmitter that creates a feeling of satisfaction in the body

serotonin toxicity　a form of drug poisoning from medications that raise serotonin levels to levels that can cause fever, rapid heart rate, muscle spasms, and even death

sleep paralysis　a phenomenon that occurs when a person is conscious but unable to move the body

solvent　a substance that can mix and dissolve another liquid, gas, or solid

synergistic effect　a physiological result when two drugs, such as alcohol and Rohypnol, are taken together

trafficked　illegally and secretly traded

Xyrem　brand name for the drug sodium oxybate, used to treat excessive daytime sleepiness and cataplexy in narcoleptics

Bibliography

Anonymous. "Using GHB to Mitigate Opiate Withdrawal." *The New Lycaeum,* September 21, 2000. http://www.lycaeum.org/leda/docs/10243.shtml?id+10243.

Bartsch, Christine, Manfred Ribe, Harald Schutz, Nikola Weigand, and Gunter Weiler. "Munchausen Syndrome by Proxy (MSBP): An Extreme Form of Child Abuse with a Special Forensic Challenge." *Forensic Science International* 137 (2003): 147–151.

Bowery, N.G. and T.G. Smart. "GABA and Glycine as Neurotransmitters: A Brief History." *British Journal of Pharmacology* 147 (2006): S109–S119.

Cohn, Michael. "GHB and Alcoholism." *The New Lycaeum.* http://www.lycaeum.org/~ghbfaq/alcoholism.html (accessed May 2, 2010).

Cottrell, A., R. Athreeres, P. Weinstock, K. Warren, and D. Gillatt. "Urinary Tract Disease Associated with Chronic Ketamine Use." *British Medical Journal* 336 (2008): 973.

Dehlin, O., M.D., R. Rubin, M.D., and A. Rundgren, M.D. "Double-blind Comparison of Zopiclone and Flunitrazepam in Elderly Insomniacs with Special Focus on Residual Effects." *Current Medical Research and Opinion* 13, 6 (1995): 317–324.

Erdely, Sabrina R. "10 Women Charged Him with Drugging and Sex Attacks, But Juries Said No," *Self,* November 21, 2008. http://www.msnbc.msn.com/id/27825997.

Forrester, Mathias B. "Flunitrazepam Abuse and Malicious Use in Texas, 1998–2003." *Substance Use and Misuse,* 41 (2006): 297–306.

Fuller, David E., Carl S. Hornfeldt, Judy S. Kelloway, Pamela J. Stahl, and Todd F. Anderson. "The Xyrem Risk Management Program." *Drug Safety* 27, 5 (2004): 293–306.

Fuller, David E., M.D., and Carl S. Hornfeldt. "Alternative Viewpoints: From Club Drug to Orphan Drug: Sodium Oxybate (Xyrem) for the Treatment of Cataplexy." *Pharmacotherapy* 23, 4 (2003): 1205.

Grootveld, Martin, Deborah Algeo, Christopher Silwood, John C. Blackburn, and Anthony D. Clark. "Determination of the Illicit Drug Gamma-hydroxybutyrate (GHB) in Human Saliva and Beverages by H NMR Analysis." *BioFactors* 27 (2006): 121–136.

Henkel, John. "Buying Drugs Online: It's Convenient and Private, but Beware of 'Rogue Sites.'" *FDA Consumer*. http://www.fda.gov/FDAC/features/2000/100_online.html (accessed November 15, 2008).

Kintz, Pascal. "Bioanalytical procedures for detection of chemical agents in hair in the case of drug-facilitated crimes." *Analytical and Bioanalytical Chemistry* 388 (2007): 1469.

Krupitsky, E.A., T. Burakov, I. Romanova, et al. "Ketamine Psychotherapy for Heroin Addiction: Immediate Effects and Two-year Follow-up." *Journal of Substance Abuse and Treatment* 23, 4 (2002): 273–283.

Lee, Steven, M.D., and Petros Levounis, M.D. "Gamma Hydroxybutyrate: An Ethnographic Study of Recreational Use and Abuse." *Journal of Psychoactive Drugs* 40, 3 (2008): 245–253.

Madea, Burkhard, and Frank Musshoff. "Knock-out Drugs: Their Prevalence, Modes of Action, and Means of Detection." *Deutsches Aerzteblatt International* 106, 20 (2009): 341–347.

Morgan, Celia J., Leslie Muetzelfeldt, Valerie Curran. "Consequences of Chronic Ketamine Self-administration upon Neurocognitive Function and Psychological Well-being: A 1-year Longitudinal Study." *Addiction* 105, 121 (2009): 1360.

Muir, David, and Miguel Sancho. "The Multiple Identities—and Crimes—of Jeffrey Marsalis," *ABC News*, July 13, 2009. http://abcnews.go.com/Primetime/story?id=8043012&page=1.

National Institute on Drug Abuse/National Institutes of Health. "Hallucinogens: LSD, Peyote, Psilocybin, and PCP." *NIDA InfoFacts*, updated June 2009. http://www.drugabuse.gov/infofacts/hallucinogens.html.

National Institutes of Health/National Institute on Drug Abuse. *Principles of Drug Addiction Treatment: A Research Based Guide*. http://www.nida.nih.gov/podat/podatindex.html (accessed May 24, 2010).

Negrusz, Adam, and R.E. Gaensslen. "Analytical Developments in Toxicological Investigation of Drug-facilitated Sexual Assault." *Analytical and Bioanalytical Chemistry* 376 (2003): 1192–1197.

Olson, James, M.D. *Clinical Pharmacology Made Ridiculously Simple*. Miami, Fla.: MedMaster, 1995.

Porrata, Trinka. "Ketamine." The GHB Project. http://www.projectghb.org/2008/ketamine.php (accessed May 1, 2010).

Ramachandran, Vilayanur, and Diane Rogers-Ramachandran. "Hey, Is That Me Over There?" *Scientific American*, April 13, 2010. http://www.scientificamerican.com/article.cfm?id=hey-is-that-me-over-there.

Saum, Christine, and James A. Inciardi. "Rohypnol Misuse in the United States." *Substance Use and Misuse* 32, 6 (1997): 724.

Schwartz, Richard, M.D., and Regina Milteer, M.D. "Drug-facilitated Sexual Assault." *Southern Medical Journal* 93, 6 (2000): 558–561.

Trevor, Anthony J., Bertram G. Katzung, and Susan B. Masters. *Katzung and Trevor's Pharmacology*. 7th ed. New York: McGraw-Hill, 2006.

U.S. Department of Justice/National Drug Intelligence Center. "GHB Analogs: GBL, BD, GHV, and GVL." *Information Bulletin,* Product No. 2002-L0424-003. August 2002.

Vastag, Brian. "Pay Attention: Ritalin Acts Much Like Cocaine." *Journal of the American Medical Association* 286, 8 (2001): 905–906.

Further Resources

Books

Dye, Christina, and Susan Mercie. *Date Rape: Unmixing Messages.* Tempe, Ariz.: Do It Now Foundation, 2009.

Icon Health Publications. *The Official Patient's Sourcebook on Rohypnol Dependence: A Revised and Updated Directory for the Internet Age.* San Diego, Calif.: Icon Health Publications, 2002.

Jansen, Karl. *Ketamine: Dreams and Realities.* Santa Cruz, Calif.: MAPS, 2004.

Porrata, Trinka. *G'd Up 24/7: The GHB Addiction Guide.* San Clemente, Calif.: Law Tech Publishing, 2007.

Koh, Me Ra. *Beauty Restored: Finding Life and Hope after Date Rape.* Ventura, Calif.: Regal Books, 2004.

Web Sites

Drug Digest
http://www.drugdigest.org

eMedicineHealth
http://www.emedicinehealth.com

The Mayo Clinic
http://www.mayoclinic.com

Partnership for a Drug-Free America
http://www.drugfree.org

Project GHB
http://www.projectghb.org

Science Daily
http://www.sciencedaily.com

U.S. Food and Drug Administration (FDA)
http://www.fda.gov

U.S. National Library of Medicine—National Institutes of Health
http://www.nlm.nih.gov

WebMD
http://www.webmd.com

Index

About the Author

Suellen May is a writer living with her son, Nathan, in Fort Collins, Colorado. She received a B.S. from the University of Vermont and an M.S. from Colorado State University. She writes science-related books and magazine articles. She is the author of *Weight-Loss Drugs, Botox and Other Cosmetic Drugs,* a five-book environmental series titled *Invasive Species,* and a forthcoming book, *Ritalin and Related Drugs.*

About the Consulting Editor

Consulting editor **David J. Triggle, Ph.D.,** is a SUNY Distinguished Professor and the University Professor at the State University of New York at Buffalo. These are the two highest academic ranks of the university. Professor Triggle received his education in the United Kingdom with a Ph.D. degree in chemistry at the University of Hull. Following post-doctoral fellowships at the University of Ottawa (Canada) and the University of London (United Kingdom) he assumed a position in the School of Pharmacy at the University at Buffalo. He served as chairman of the Department of Biochemical Pharmacology from 1971 to 1985 and as dean of the School of Pharmacy from 1985 to 1995. From 1996 to 2001 he served as dean of the Graduate School and from 1999 to 2001 was also the University Provost. He is currently the University Professor, in which capacity he teaches bioethics and science policy, and is president of the Center for Inquiry Institute, a think tank located in Amherst, New York, and devoted to issues around the public understanding of science. In the latter respect he is a major contributor to the online M.Ed. program—"Science and The Public"—in the Graduate School of Education and The Center for Inquiry.